Welcome to Earth

a book of peace by John Gihair

Welcome to Earth

A healthy expansion into transcendental development

Copyright © Ranjinder Singh Gihair 2015

The right of Ranjinder Singh Gihair to be identified as the Author of the Work has been asserted by him in accordance with sections 77 and 78 of the Copyright, Designs and Patents Act 1988.

All rights reserved. No part of this publication may be reproduced, stored in a retrieval system, or transmitted, in any form or by any means without the prior written permission of the publisher, nor be otherwise circulated in any form of binding or cover other than that in which it is published and without a similar condition being imposed on the subsequent purchaser.

A mutual Disclaimer agreed upon the purchase of this book, 'Welcome to Earth' that duty of care and attention prevents unreasonable risk of harm or injury. To ignore these principles is at your own risk.

John Gihair

About the Author

It is easy to open a door, but a door that has been opened for you, that has *torn* through the fabric of your known reality so you can be seen and heard, is that of a great strength, a great gift and a great belonging.

Contents

Acknowledgements	ix
Introduction	xi
Forward	xiii
Awareness	1
Cycles	4
Improper Cycles	5
Understanding DNA	7
Connecting to the Universe	10
The Earth's Electromagnetic field	12
Electromagnetic Spectrum, Gravity and Balance	14
The Universe at Large	18
Earth Chakras and Energy Points	21
Vision Board	25
Human Chakras	28
Feng Shui	33
Balance	37
Follow the Light	41
The Great OM	44
Linguistics	50
Mythical Metamorphosis	52
Emitting Emotions	56
Helping your Higher Self	58
Incarnation, Magic and Imagination	60
Love is Life	65
The Battle for Your Higher Self	68
Realisation	71
Each Energy Point Has Its Own Characters	74
Sexual Meditation	81
Sacrifice	83
Chi	91
Breathing	93

Channelling Energy using Mirrors into Your Being	97
The Phoenix	102
Sins of the Mind	109
Water	130
Bibliography	138
Index	140

Acknowledgements

Great Spirit, how can I thank you enough! Please let my lifetime speak of gratitude for having being gifted the acknowledgment of you, the acknowledgement of my parents and this ancient blood that runs through these veins of mine.

This hand might have swirled around in a pattern creating these English letters that form these sentences, but by no means did the information come from my conscious mind at the time. The Will of a thought created the pieces to the jigsaw puzzle that so happened to transform into the scriptures that reside within these pages to follow. Humble thanks to a man who stuck by me, throughout this transcendental expansion of awakening consciousness, for his patience and curious nature to see where these pieces to the puzzle came from, and formed as I embodied on my quest around the globe to find my life manual. Thank you to my researcher Shane Moore for tip-toeing the edge of the expanding creation with me.

Thank you to professional, scientific breakthroughs that I have incorporated into my works, friends for taking the time to create such art within the world. Thank you for proofreading my work, giving an honest analysis.

Thank you to Jiayi Li, Chinese Translator, for guiding my safe passage throughout China.

A stature of character with a steadfast approach to collaborating and designing the front cover of this book and several digital photos within the chapters that are to follow. Thank you Sandeep Daley for stepping into my world and blessing me with your talents, heart and soul.

Thank you to Hitz Rao, friend, photographer of the photos within these chapters. In my eyes a photographer has the perception that is subject to interpretation to collaborated finishings. A photographer with such qualities that promote inspiration and is personally driven to tune into the artist and then express and deliver. Hitz Rao is naturally like this.

A healthy thank you to Lawrence Smith, Managing Director from Snappy Snaps Birmingham UK. Without Lawrence I wouldn't have found Sandeep. Designer of the front cover of 'Welcome to Earth' and other images found throughout the many chapters. Lawrence and his team. Marvin Alexander, Cristina Cochior and Vlad Costache had my best intentions held in their unconditional continual support.

Thank you to Paul Manning, Nick Du Boulay (Image Engineer) and Matt Crisp from Blue Cedar Print Works Glastonbury UK. My gratitude for Paul's fresh eyes and keen enthusiasm to mass produce this book, for going beyond to self-publish this book on Amazon; keeping this vision and inspiration alive.

Thank you to Samir Bhamra, Creative Director for the Collaborated photos within these pages. This man is a true all-rounder that touched such areas as stage setting, castings, international involvements, handling documentations etc. With the foreseeable ability to know the artists individual exact needs, so the artist can continue to expand into consciousness.

Thank you to Lucan Jackson for the illustration throughout. Thank you, for at a moment's notice, dropping everything, staying up until 4am to produce inspired image's that I became aware of through meditation.

Thank you to Buddha Maitreya at Pure land meditation centre and Japanese Garden for your perception and use of your gardens.

Thank you to Wollaton Hall for such hospitality in inviting us to your location and grounds for parts for this project, Welcome to Earth.

Thank you to the Royal Shakespeare Company for props and intrigue.

Thank you to the Mercure Grand Hotel in inviting us to your location for parts for this project, Welcome to Earth.

Thank you to Prabhjot Hunjan for giving me light when it was dark.

Thank you to Models. Caroline Nicolai Bruhn, Sara Aras, Josie Merchan Annabel Mizel, and Prabhjot Hunjan for bringing and sharing parts of this vision.

Thank you to Tee Jay for the CGI image. Your effort while under pressure from graduation is a sure sign of commitment.

Thank you to InkTree for printing the door-to-door promotional flyers.

Thank you to Neil Cotton for your support toward promoting the book, for a comfortable place to hold innovating meetings and for the lovely food.

Thank you to Phlik Make Up for your skilled art of makeup, hair and attention to detail, for such prophetic, realistic makeup regarding the Dog-eat-Dog art piece.

Thank you to Ian Hawksford, Salon Director from Costello's for all the male hair styling and chats.

Thank you to Alex Copp and Lawrence Smith for taking it upon themselves to finalize stages of the finishing project, 'Welcome to Earth'. You both couldn't have helped at a better time, thank you for being there.

Thank you to Holly, my good friend, cat model for your unconditional love.

Paintings, male model, commissioner, Author, John Gihair

Introduction

In early March 2011, I embarked upon a journey that set my gaze, 'stood at the top of the great Andes in Peru.' Leaving the last village, the point of no return, we pack our tents and other belongings and set off toward the mountains' pass. The team and I walk through lands of new, timely rests where pools of ice tell the story of moving into another biosphere. The land underfoot started to turn into a glacier as we ascended the mountains' passages. The expedition leader mentioned previously while at base camp "take a stone as an offering to the God's of the mountain". With fresh eyes and frozen vapour on my face we stood facing where we had just travelled. I hold the stone in prayer-like hands now that we had reached the summit of the mountain. The wind blew calmly and suddenly. There were many stones placed upon one another, like totem poles as memorials to surviving adventurers such as myself. Placing my stone I was grounded and I looked hastily around, excited in the notion of descending the second largest mountain in the known world. I searched for wood, anything to make a sledge or skies. In my excitement I only see stone upon stones. Steadying myself for a second I look to my chest. I am wearing a gore-tex jacket I think to myself and smile. "Okay," I said to the team members, "I am off!" They look at me in humour. "What do you mean you are off?" With that I leap off the mountain's peak onto the glacier snow, sliding on my belly as the first human to surf down this mountain in a gore-tex jacket. The expedition leader later explains that this mountain hasn't had snow on it for 35 years as I keenly acknowledge his words. Surfing down the mountain I found myself funnelled into a valley to where a slowly forming river had been created by the erosion. Gradually the sides of the river banks grew larger and so did the smile on my face. Thrilled to be bobsledding through this frozen river on my belly I cry and laugh and giggle at this unforgettable experience. I climb the bank of the river in total celebration as I look up to small dots that are the team descending the mountain. Covered in snow I look around to a lake that once was beneath me.

The scene was rocky with many coloured grasses surrounding the lake. A path to my left led down to where wild horses grazed at the water's edge, but my attention was to my right where a magnificent wild white horse stood alone. I slowly took my backpack off and laid it on a rock as I humbly walked several steps toward the horse. Kneeling, I looked into the horse's eyes and a moment is shared, a moment where all restrictions seemed to pass unseen. There wasn't any judgment, only truth in this timeless place. Our time lasted and then I asked if I can take a photo in memory. The horse bowed her head, raising it, she bellows a plume of steam out of her nose with the look of acceptance as I wasn't just a bystander at this point, I had become a part of the land.

In this moment I look up to my right, sensing a magical movement coming from above the top of the mountain's peak, a feeling, *a frequency*, a moving entity. I didn't know what I had witnessed until months later after writing a book, *this book* of consciousness. I wasn't aware that I was writing a book of what I experienced in that exact moment! This book was written through me!

The pages that are to follow took me five months to write and a further two and a half years to refine as my consciousness wasn't aware of what I was writing. This book is a mind-map that is, for the most part autobiographical so please read beginning to end, be gentle and kind to yourself as you venture into my world. The scientific knowledge is brief and will help bring peace and hopefully humour to the logical mind, expanding into the illogical mind, imagination, mystery, magic, transcendental development resulting in *quantum leaping through conscious tunnelling*. There are many activities within this book or journey itself, so please participate in action. Alternatively, just reading the scriptures will satisfy.

I do indeed wish you a comfortable read ahead. This book, my journey across the great continents of this beautiful, habitable planet Earth was in search of my life's manual. Truth be told, the initial thought of desire is the start and the finishing line. *There is no separation.* It's only the journey toward the so called finish that can spin us into a beehive.

My warmest appreciation.
John Gihair

Forward

(Forward by Shane Moore, co Alex Copp)

In the Kabbalah, one of the oldest of Religions has one of the most logical explanations for its beginnings with which I give a very simplified version. Once there was pure complete energy. At some time it made a vessel. The vessel started to receive all the energy yet, in its nature, wished to share its energy and made other vessels. The pure energy could never be extinguished. It is all things and yet to be all things and returns to origin.

You could say the vessel is the universe, the Big Bang its creation. Stars formed and then exploded. The contents of the stars produced more complex particles. This process repeats ad infinitum even to this day; to make planets, to make solar systems, to make galaxies. Given enough time and space, anything can be made from the smallest of starts. All things are made of stars. You are made of stardust. We are stars who have achieved sentience. The children of the Big Bang, one big intergalactic family.

Then some fundamental basics came into play called the 4 Laws of Thermodynamics, contributed to by a number of scientists: Anders Celsius, Daniel Gabriel Fahrenheit, Jacques Alexandre César Charles, Robert Boyle, Johannes Diderik Van der Waals, Lord Kelvin, Ludwig Boltzmann, Maxwell, Einstein, Bose, Fermi, Dirac, Willard Gibbs, James Joule, Helmholtz and Sterling.

The 4 laws are outlined below:

Zeroth Law of Thermodynamics: where two objects in thermal equilibrium with a third object are in equilibrium with each other. It is the most fundamental law. All things seek to be in balance with one another. Additionally, all things want to get back to their original potential.

It is named the 0th law due to it being discovered last, however it is more fundamental than the 1st law.

First Law of Thermodynamics, or the Law of the Conservation of Energy: all energy cannot be created or destroyed, it merely changes form. The energy in a closed system remains constant. So the Universe's energy is constant, it is impossible to get more energy out of a system than is in it. We have a concept of how much energy is in the universe from obvious sources. We can get more efficiency by putting work into a system. If you put more order into a system, the system performs more orderly. If you introduce chaos into a system, the system performs chaotically (Chaos Theory, the Butterfly Effect, ongoing work since Isaac Newton, Oestreicher 2007).

Second Law of Thermodynamics: heat always flows towards a cold object. This is called Entropy, which is the measure of thermal energy that becomes unavailable to work as mechanical energy. Entropy can also be interpreted as the amount of randomness or disorder in a system.

Third Law of Thermodynamics: when a system reaches absolute zero, it's entropy reaches zero. When all heat is removed, all forces between energies organise when there is no motion. It is impossible to remove all heat from a system as all things are in motion therefore generating heat.

Regarding the actual entire energy of the universe, we don't know how much there is even with the knowledge of Einstein's infamous equation of $E=mc^2$. This includes our own human energy systems, the systems we create and exert control over like stock markets, and systems we depend upon such as the weather.

We don't know. That should be every human credo. We do not have 100% knowledge on everything and there is no absolute answer for everything.

We don't know why we sleep. We don't know what electric is. Gravity is a fundamental force in nature and there is no real understanding of it. We cannot even locate 96% of the universe. We know that 4% of it is matter, or energy, that makes us physical. Twenty-three percent is Dark Matter which is a force that is invisible yet reacts to gravity and glues matter together. Seventy-three percent is Dark Energy, another force that eludes us yet expands the universe. All models of the universe that are run through super computers without the 96% of its darkness just do not work.

It gets even better. Of the 4% which is the arch of relativity we can actively interact with, we experience even less than 0.1%!

Such luminary figures as Newton and Spinoza researched heavily into the Kabbalah. Dmitri Mendeleev drew inspiration from the religious text, The Zohar. He later dreamt of the Periodic Table. This table gave birth to basic understandings of our world. Religion has fed science many times and science has informed religion.

Human nature, indeed the laws of nature, wish to bestow knowledge or information onto the next generation for bettering itself. Life, it seems, is in competition with life. How many abstract examples of this have we seen through history?

In all cultures, religions and philosophy, the beginning of life has always been the number one question. We, as individuals, always come to one point in our lives with the big questions: How? Why? When? Who?

Abiogenesis is the scientific explanation for the origin of life. The laws of thermodynamics have never been conclusive in reaching an answer for spontaneous life. With regard to the 2nd Law, it would mean more work would have to be created out of energy that was not there or the laws lack the sufficient reasons for the occurrence of life. This is a common misinterpretation. Multiple experiments throughout the ages tried to find empirical proof for life from nothingness but to no avail. Other theories emerged from lightning striking a puddle of mud. Of course Creationists claimed this as God's intervention.

Dr Jack Szostak, Laureate Nobel Prize Winner for Psychology and Medicine, found in multiple experiments that basic elements that would have been found on a very young Earth, if left alone in the right environment, would start to organically link together to form the very first building blocks of life. These very simple molecular machines would absorb others, self replicate and become more ordered in their evolution over time and eventually become more complex, eventually giving birth to self aware life.

The inventor of Wolfram Alpha, Stephen Wolfram has designed a website that computes any question you give it. From things as simple as "1+2", "how many stars in the galaxy" to "math of the trefoil knot" it not only gives the result, also all information relevant to it, graphs, pictures etc and suggestions. During his TED talk "Computation for the Theory of Everything" he explains something he coins "Computational Irreducibility". This is where he shows incredibly simple systems can produce extremely complex sophisticated systems that naturally occur beyond predictability of scientific study. The universe has this in abundance, integrating what is within it into its systems and creates or plays with what it has. This is the limit of our control over finite systems, including the ones we create such as the trade system, progress of technology, biological processes, even human evolution is also under the big question mark of predictability. We have to watch its growth and give into to the power of not knowing.

So given enough time, the right space and correct ingredients, similar to the early nature of stardust creating planets, Life can be so.

Leonardo Fibonacci's infamous Fibonacci Sequence is probably the most important and simple mathematics in the universe. It is the foundation for the Golden Ratio, The Golden Swirl, The Golden Mean. It is the middle way of mathematics to have beauty and truth for one was deemed inseparable from the other. It is the sequence any child can play by adding the number before to get the next number starting from 1: 0, 1, 1, 2, 3, 5, 8, 13, 21, 34, 55, 89, 144, 233, 377 and so forth.

The Golden Ratio is expressed as A + B is to A as A is to B. For example the number 3 has the relation of 1+2 as 2 has the relation of 1+1. This can also be mathematically expressed as 1.6180339887 recurring.

This relation can be found virtually everywhere, the spiral in sea shells, the building proportions of the Great Pyramids, the growth of plants, human DNA, crystal structures etc. Adolf Zeising found the Golden Ratio to be a universal law and wrote "in which is contained the ground-principle of all formative striving for beauty and completeness in the realms of both nature and art, and which permeates, as a paramount spiritual ideal, all structures, forms and proportions, whether cosmic or individual, organic or inorganic, acoustic or optical; which finds it's fullest realisation, however, in the human form."

Another famous Leonardo Da Vinci, found inherent beauty and complexity in the Golden Ratio. Da Vinci was trying to find the maths in man and to take on the challenge of squaring the circle. He created the world famous Vitruvian Man, and in the proportions of man he found the Golden Ratio so many times over it was undeniable to him that man was in part nature's design and the inherent symmetry of the universe.

From the Laws of Thermodynamics, various religious decrees, philosophical reasoning, economics, and the understanding of nature there is a truth. We are the architects and adolescents of order and chaos, and the only power we have is choice. Ultimately all energy is information exchange and representation of a system. We are the energy that can choose to change the energy we receive, give and take. It is the governing of balance that is our true challenge.

(Forward, by Shane Moore
co Alex Copp.)

Awareness

I would like to start by saying that the majority of the images and personalities that you are holding in your mind are not yours, or you, they never were. Most of the images that you are holding are inherited from perpetual harmonic cycles that your parents and ancestors could not break, forming into defence mechanisms. The other images we hold are that of mass media, manifested into the outer-self. A very small percentage of expressional images that you hold are yours, but we only consciously release them into fruition for short periods of the day because media and predecessor energy has our energetic emotions running a dance.

To learn how to manifest, we first must learn how to govern our emotions and not let them be governed by opposing ones any further.

Our time in this conscious realm is limited, so don't let yourself be a slave to your false major, minor and micro personalities any longer. To fuse synthetic unity, creating a state where all of our personalities harmoniously co-exist, rather than allowing them to live with rebellion, is a choice we can and do make.

Cycles of behaviour are but fears, lowly energetic emotions that we can and will break through with the understanding on how to govern ourselves and not let other worlds control us. We are also driven by our higher selves, our higher planes of service. These pathways of ancestral energies know how to guide us. If we can stay within the correct flow of emotional energy with heart we can indeed move rapidly towards what we see fit as 'conscious treasure' and honour the truth of our true identity.

We have now come to a time in this dimension where we have the knowledge and conscious power to use our higher selves for greater practice for the unity of all realms.

My beliefs are not to focus just on the scientific rule of law within the universe; I believe you should infuse your chosen religious spiritual beliefs with findings that I will explain in this book, to give you a greater understanding, and to empower your spiritual religious beliefs by discovering deeper messages that already exist within your chosen manuscripts.

Throughout time there has been a recurring story, a story that has basic laws. We have used these laws in countless fiction: action, romance, religious euphoria, but all have the basic laws. We have learnt from great minds such as the Elders, Albert Einstein, Max Planck, Steven Hawking, etc. that this is an orderly universe thus rules are there to follow. These laws can be, and are used, for control or for compassion. We use these laws everyday on a miniscule scale and on a much larger scale. The divine laws are all around us, you just have to open your eyes of mind and heart to see anew!

We are led to believe that all the great answers are but lost to our conscious mind and history. This is a lie because if we believe that the answers are lost, then they indeed will be lost as the mind and heart become limited.

Throughout my search around the world of the so called *lost*, I found myself on an internal journey, battling for control over my energetic emotional personalities that were formed as major and minor selves. I found in South America that the clarity of the great Andes brought forth images and sentences of the long forgotten past-times. This place, with its breath-taking scenes and what seemed to be endless trekking, activated my awareness.

Peru and Bolivia had a lasting impact on me, so much so that the vibration bestowed upon that great continent ignited a different pathway of thought, fusing an expansion in my not so conscious awareness! Travelling the routes that this continent planned, I often met people along the way. Their intercontinental laughter and cultural habits were strong in character but less in understanding. When approaching these people, I quickly realised that they had answers on how to govern my energetic emotions of heart. What a strange revelation I thought to myself. Reflecting on what had gripped me so, I started rewinding my life story. There were so many similarities that it kept me up for several nights, pondering on what seemed to be a DVD playing over and over.

My life couldn't possibly be a repeating like an episode of The Last of the Summer Wine, but it was! I was, and had been, living in limbo, doomed to live the same emotional 'selves' over and over again! How could this even be possible? I thought. Yes the images had changed and I hadn't had any pressure off my peers - or had I? I pressured myself so the emotions were still there, along with most of the others I recalled, just in a different format in perception of reality. The life that I had been living hadn't changed emotionally for as long as I could remember.

I stood facing the mirror in my hotel room, reassuring myself that humans are creatures of habit, so as not to fall into despair as my eyes gazed into the abyss. Suddenly, I focussed upon a photograph on the mirror of myself as a teenager, a snippet of history where I had been captured sleeping with beer cans abundantly littering the scene. I drew my look back to the mirror. The man that I gazed upon was gazing back at me shouting the words "Evolutionary Frequencies".

I had read about these evolutional frequency patterns but had never pushed the idea. Seemingly, to find them automatically took me by surprise. I guess believing is seeing. Promptly, and with probably too much haste to break my emotional cycles, I had reacted to what I thought to be a personal revelation which became a natural phenomenon.

Cycles

While in Peru, I came across a beautifully built church that housed quite a number of interesting paintings such as the generic paintings of Jesus and the horrific judgment he endured. Funnily enough, and to my surprise, I looked at these paintings completely differently. What if all these paintings are metaphors? Yes of course they are, I thought, kicking myself. What if the cross symbolised the baggage that people carried throughout life? It dawned on me that this information could keep people in bondage, or free them. I continued to shift into the shadows as the guards didn't take kindly to my over-fascination with these beautifully illustrated paintings. Another painting caught my innocent eye. This painting was immediately aware of itself, a painting with such presence but found in the most unlikely of places. I stared at the towering black shadow that loomed over Jesus while he knelt looking up. A thought rushed across my mind while I myself looked up. The thought was that of perpetual cycles! What does this mean? I thought.

We are born into a particular 'curriculum' that is set by the old conscious self-indoctrinated by our grand-parents and so forth. These mind-sets are our building blocks of energy. We had to come from somewhere and we came from them. This is why we must know about our past before we can move on with our futures. By knowing this, we choose to live in the present.

While my time was pressured, as the advancing guard approached, I noticed the melody playing on the organ through the fingers of a devotee. The sound waves that were carrying across the air particles pierced my body with the vibrations of surrendering to their tree of life!

Our inherited energies are our black shadows that loom over us. We learn through self-sacrifice or proving identity to evolve, that is the realm. We all go through times of self-discovery and we all go through times of highs and lows. The question is why. Why do we need the highs and lows? Why do we need the self-discovery? We are but a composite of energy. Our direct forms of energy were generated from that of our Mother and that of our Father, thus we were incubated and grew on one level of reality.

Improper Cycles

Through past evolution we have been fighting a strong adversary – this is our animalistic side in action. To be able to ascend into higher reaches of vibrational existence this side of us needs peace because we live within the 21st century! To subconsciously, or consciously, fight this powerful heritage of survival and competitive race to sow our seed we relinquish our higher selves.

When we eat heavy foods like meat, a conscious living being activates these 'hunter' chemicals thus empowering our primal self and slowing the energy of lighter ascensions. This also desensitises us as, if not taught, we lose the compassion and respect for other beings that live in harmony on Mother Earth. To work towards our higher selves we must starve this powerful ancient side.

Brain tissue is metabolically expensive. The often-cited relationship between diet and relative brain size is more properly viewed as a relationship between relative brain size and relative gut size, the latter determined by dietary quality. "No matter what is selecting for relatively large brains in humans and other primates, they cannot be achieved without a shift to a high-quality diet unless there is a rise in the metabolic rate. Therefore the incorporation of increasingly greater amounts of animal products into the diet was essential in the evolution of the large human brain." *(Leslie C. Aiello, 1995)*

Yes, consuming animal produce may well have played a vital part in the vast array of nutrients needed to evolve but we are not limited to our current environment any longer as an evolved, adapting species. We have the world's foods at our doorstep, many protein products that will cater for your needs, and all the literature and means to live within the correct balance, or chosen reality.

Carnivores and vegetarians are that of different fashions, resulting in different conscious outcomes of light works or art expressed.

"A toxic person generally has an acidic pH level that results from the ingestion of animal proteins, refined sugars and cooked fats. These foods are poorly digested and create toxic residues which are then absorbed into the bloodstream. Conversely, the more alkaline the body, the more serene or calm the individual. Increased intake of living foods (fruits and vegetables) helps to create an alkaline pH level."(Vegetarianism, Mental Benefits. www.celestialhealing.net)

Fresh raw foods are needed to supply the body with essential elements not available in cooked, processed food.

The 2010 version of Dietary Guidelines for Americans, a report issued every five years by the U.S. Department of Agriculture and the U.S. Department of Health and Human Services states:

"In prospective studies of vegetarians, compared to non-vegetarian eating patterns, vegetarian-style eating patterns have been associated with

improved health outcomes—lower levels of obesity, a reduced risk of cardiovascular disease, and lower total mortality. Several clinical trials have documented that vegetarian eating patterns lower blood pressure.

On average, vegetarians consume a lower proportion of calories from fat (particularly saturated fatty acids); fewer overall calories; and more fibre, potassium, and vitamin C than do non-vegetarians. Vegetarians generally have a lower body mass index. These characteristics and other lifestyle factors associated with a vegetarian diet may contribute to the positive health outcomes that have been identified among vegetarians."

As we suppress parts of ourselves to accommodate the social acceptance of living within a society, we lose parts of ourselves. By suppressing anger and rage emotions we take that part of ourselves away that can cause trauma to the body. By learning dietary solutions to be able to conform within society, and leave the primal self forever we can, of course, not suppress but release this hunger/ thirst type of appetite.

Understanding DNA

DNA is the carrier of our genetic information and is passed down from generation to generation. All of the cells in our bodies, except red blood cells, contain a copy of our DNA. All life is a process of information exchange.

Since its discovery by Crick and Watson, the DNA double helix has become known as the template of all life forms and has been around in science for some fifty years now. Our knowledge about DNA since then has dramatically increased. Of the complete chain of triplets in a complete DNA string only 5% is used for coding and the reproduction of proteins; the other 95% is dormant DNA.

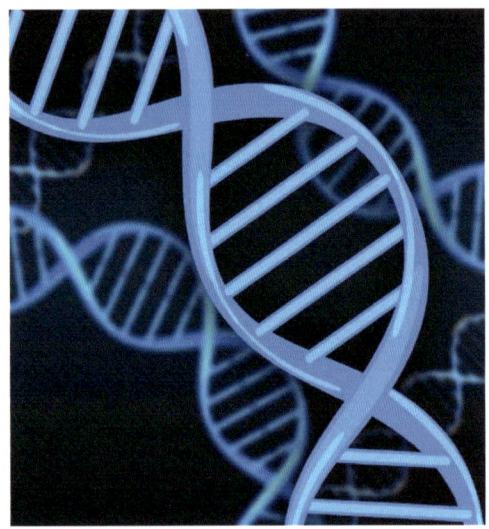

Revolutionary new discoveries revealed that the idea that the inherited genetic makeup of an organism cannot be changed is wrong. It has been proven that the sequence of DNA molecule's codons can be reprogrammed. The codons of the DNA string can be rearranged in different sequences. In other words, the software of the human genome, our DNA molecules, can be reprogrammed. Research reveals that the triplets in the DNA string are able to exchange places.

Here are some excerpts from Jan Wicherinks work 'The Mysterious DNA':

"The most astonishing experiment that was performed by Garjajev's group is the reprogramming of the DNA codon sequences using modulated laser light. From their discovered grammatical syntax of the DNA language they were able to modulate coherent laser light and even radio waves and add semantics (meaning) to the carrier wave. In this way they were able to reprogram in vivo DNA in living organisms, by using the correct resonant frequencies of DNA."

"The most impressive discovery made so far is that spoken language can be modulated to the carrier wave with the same reprogramming effect. Now this is a baffling and stunning scientific discovery! Our own DNA can simply be reprogrammed by human speech, supposing that the words (chants etc) are modulated on the correct carrier frequencies."

"Whereas western science uses complicated bio chemical processes to cut and paste DNA triplets in the DNA molecule, Russian scientists use modulated laser light to do exactly the same thing. The Russians have proven to be very successful in repairing damaged DNA material in vivo."

"Laser light therapies based on Garjajev's findings are already applied in some European academic hospitals with success on various sorts of skin cancer. The cancer is cured without any remaining scars." (Wicherink, 2006).

Emotions

"Daniel Winter and his heart coherence team have found proof that human emotions can reprogram DNA as well. The sonic beatings of the heart in rhythm with our feelings, our emotions, are transformed into electromagnetic energy in the body's glands that act like piezoelectric couplers creating smaller electromagnetic counterpart wavelengths of the emotional sounds of the heart. The emotion becomes energy in motion, e-motion, sending it right down to the DNA of every cell of our body as blue coherent laser light that is able to modulate the DNA codons just like the lasers of the Russians did."

"The DNA molecule as a wave shape is attuned to the heart and able to receive its sonic emotions. Daniel Winter explains the implosion of long waves into short waves as the mechanism that conveys the emotions of the heart to our DNA. The scale (wavelength) is different but the ratio of the wavelengths is the same maintaining the Golden Mean ratio."

"Not only do emotions feed our DNA with blue ultraviolet light, but also cellular metabolism, the consumption of food, is all about creating short wave blue light that feeds our DNA. Plants receive this light directly from the Sun, using chlorophyll in their leaves and use a process called photosynthesis to bind the photons of the Sun."

"Mammals consuming these plants get these bio photons indirectly from plants, the accumulation however has become less effective. Eventually the coherent light of the Sun is stored as bio photons in the organism. The purpose of the metabolisms in both plants and mammals is to create highly coherent ultraviolet laser light inside the DNA that drives cell replication."

"DNA's purpose is not to serve solely as a chemical memory device for the reproduction of proteins. Russian research has revealed that we have underestimated the intelligence of DNA as it acts like a bio computer, and is able to process biological information of the cell metabolism that takes place in our body."

"Most astonishing, the codon sequences of DNA can be reprogrammed by coherent frequency lazar light, radio waves and Human Emotions. We have just started to discover the gateway functions of DNA to information fields, the bridge to what Rupert Sheldrake called the morphic genetic fields of life." (Wicherink, 2006)

To understand ourselves in greater depth we first must look at our outward inherited selves, our parents, as we share programmed DNA of old biological information:
- Followed behavioural patterns
- What are our parents' higher selves?
- What are their desires?
- What are their fears and conflictions?

Discovering these simplistic states through meditation takes away the need to beg the answers from reluctant or separated parents, as most of these you have already gone through, including the fears and conflictions you have just dismissed. The best way to explain this is to reflect on my own personal field test, *my life story*.

Unbeknown to myself, as I wasn't raised with a male role-model, I had already lived out my Father's lifestyle. I had also lived a number of my Mother's dreams.

Mother	M+Myself	Father	F+Myself
A beautiful woman who had the opportunity to become a model. Sadly her husband was increasingly insecure and the dream was lost because she was a traditional woman.	Driven toward self-expression, I enjoy both being in front of and behind the camera as a performer, actor and model.	My father was and still is heavily involved in movement, which takes the form of martial arts or battle strategies. He has developed his passed down Sikh heritage in the form of his own style of martial art.	Compelled to soul search for the exact movement for self-expression, I experienced many years of several styles of self-defence arts, eventually finding performance art.

This example is but a small illustration of the set, pre-programmed energetic cycle, or cycles, that we are born with. Working through each interest within your personal life story, you will find that most years are not yours. There is a saying that parents live their lives through their children. This is true, if they didn't have the strength to break or finish their cycles of desire or truth. They let other worlds interfere with their true path of harmonics.

Rebellion can take the form of the simplest of things and can stay with you for a life time, or life times! As soon as you can distinguish where your life path truly belongs, down the middle, your mother's life will fall away and so will your father's, thus your true path will be shown and the potential energy that was held back by old conscious beliefs will flow into your very existence.

Connecting to the Universe

As a young child I would often wonder why I was born into a family that were 'alternative' or out of the mainstream. Not having a normal perception, unlike the many other kids and adults around me, I soon got lost in merging my full consciousness with social acceptance. Suffering hardship in understanding conscious expansion, I often ran over to a green pasture where I found solace at the top of the hill. I remember a time when I shouted up to the thunder clouds, "I am here, it is my turn!"

What did this mean? I asked myself after the frustration subsided. What it meant was that I was trying to connect to the Universe, to my higher self. I didn't realise this until years later.

Energy passes through a massive electromagnetic field, the planet earth, and into us, empowering our own electromagnetic fields by activating our energy points (Chakras: see page, 28). This can be released out of the top of your head (your Crown Chakra) and into the universe, 'Father Sky', as an emotional electromagnetic frequency. The universe isn't biased, it is just receiving frequencies emitting from a body, either programmed by old conscious cycles inherited by our ancestors or alien images of media etc.

Connecting to the universe is a combination of letting trust of nurturing into your second sacred Sacrum Chakra and letting go of your desires and dreams through your seventh Crown Chakra. This energy flows through us but first it must be empowered by energetic emotional information. If we are lacking in this field of frequency then it's like driving a vehicle at one hundred miles per hour and having your engine seize. You would completely go out of control and come to a grinding halt.

This is why we need to connect to the planet, animal, insects, mountains, ourselves etc. and live in harmony as part of the earthly realm, Mother Earth. The more we connect to everything as one, the more we tap into the world's and universe's energy and electromagnetic fields. This universal energy enters through the Crown Chakra into the top part of our heart, our inner Father Sky. The energy from the Earth enters the earthly body through the Base Chakra into the bottom of the heart, our inner Mother Earth, bridging the realms of transcendental consciousness!

Think of the universe as a human body. Within the human body we have blood cells that fight off viruses, chemicals that create happiness, and we store photons to change our DNA. We also feed ourselves proteins to repair muscle damage and much more. All of these workings are to keep the human body in perfect working condition. Now look at the universe as a perfect working organism, where the human or living organisms are the atoms that emit the light frequency to convert the energy to the progression of the ever expanding universe.

If we can stop and realise that we are part of this perfect working network, we can learn what our part within the great chain of life is! If light energy, emotional, and energetic elemental energy ends up emitting out into space, then every action or reaction is adding to the ever expanding universe.

As you come to this realisation, doubt can form in the mind as we tend to feel insignificant compared in size.

Let me just say, size has no significance within dimensions, and that you are a very important key in the chain of life. You are life, and life is you.

To stand up and be counted is something my childhood taught me! It also taught me to be part of a social grouping, to be part of a community; to unite within my skin and feel settled beyond doubt.

The Earth's Electromagnetic field

This picture, as an example, shows the working magnetic field and planetary alignment in operation. The sun blasting its solar winds out into the vast space of this not so quiet part of the galaxy toward our habitable planet Earth.

Most of the astrophysical objects (celestial bodies) that surround us (planets, stars and galaxies) have a magnetic field, whose origin is poorly understood. Such magnetic fields can play a major role in the evolution of various structures throughout the universe. The Earth's magnetic field, which is thought to be caused by the movements of liquid ferrous iron in the outer core (assuming that the outer core is in a liquid state); not only makes compass needles point north but also protects us from the harmful effects of the cosmic rays and the solar winds from the Sun (Pétrélis 2009).

With regard to planetary alignment, magnetic fields are more important than the distribution of the masses of planets. For example, volcanic activity on the earth has been shown to be correlated with the magnetic field of Jupiter. The planet Jupiter has a very strong magnetic field and its spin axis is different to that of most of the other planets in that it is very near its orbital plane. So the changes in its magnetic field coupled to the earth and the sun are much more dramatic.

This magnetic field coupling to the sun and the earth changes over the course of the orbiting of the planets and is dependent on the magnetic field orientation of each. The changes in the magnetic fields induce changes in the solar emissions from the sun. This in turn affects many things on the earth such as communication systems, weather systems, increases the probability of earthquakes, volcanic activity, and the intensity of our own human magnetic field.

What is more important to realise is that if these planets are emitting an electromagnetic field at times where the planet is under attack from outer influences, such as solar winds, that could damage the earth, then it means that the planet itself is making a conscious decision to protect itself or herself.

The Earth's Electromagnetic Field

This is evidence that the planet is a conscious living being, which is a part of a much larger living conscious being, the Universe.

The more we, as individuals, learn about and understand the celestial bodies that orbit within our solar system, the Milky Way and other solar systems, the more we can gaze up into the infinite possibilities of expansion.

As we gaze up our bodies do one of two things. Firstly, one of the bodily senses is to sense distance. We become aware of the planet's patterns, galaxies, births of new stars and solar systems etc, we become more conscious of the outer existence of planets, galaxies and the overall expanding universe of consciousness. We forever expand as the body senses new energy within the universe, which induces growth within the soul and the connection with the divine. We experience this when a loved one gives birth to new life.

Secondly, gazing up into the array of heavenly light, we process the photons from distant planets, galaxies etc. If part of our soul search is to re-program DNA by diet, speech etc, imagine what consciousness we will obtain if we process light from distant stars (Moon bathe) that are filtered down through our retinas into the body!

The Universe at large

The Milky Way Galaxy

The feeling of expansion, coupled with acquiring more photons into our focused consciousness, Exterritorial or Earthly, is another key to awakening.

Electromagnetic Spectrum, Gravity and Balance

The Electromagnetic Spectrum (EM) is the medium in which we experience every day phenomenon. Hertz (Hz) is the measure of the number of waves that pass within a second; the longer the wave, the lower the hertz, the weaker the energy.

The electromagnetic spectrum is how we measure every single wave and particle property in our known universe. Dark Energy and Dark Matter do not interact with it, if not pure in intention! Humans, with all our senses, can experience less than around 1% of the electromagnetic spectrum itself, and that's greatly over-estimating it. To put it into perspective, if a roll of film was 2,500 miles long one frame would represent all of the visible light that we perceive.

All things, on some level, emit, absorb and reflect all levels of the EM spectrum according to their design or composition. This is their balance. A leaf, for example, will reflect the green wavelength as it is already in its system and absorb ultraviolet waves for energy and emit others. Of course if Gamma radiation were to hit the leaf due to its high intensity wave, it would kill the leaf due to overpowering its system or composition. We know this because we have developed technology to the point of detecting almost all its wavelengths. We use this knowledge for such things as MRI scans and compositions of our planet and others around us.

Gravity

Gravity moves through all dimensions and is a fundamental cause by which physical bodies attract with a force proportional to their emitting mass. In everyday life, gravity is most familiar as the agent that gives weight to objects with mass and causes them to fall to the ground when dropped.

Gravitation causes dispersed matter to attract, and matter to remain intact, thus accounting for the existence of the Earth, the Sun, and most of the objects in the universe. It is responsible for keeping the Earth and the other planets in their orbit around the Sun, for keeping the moon in its orbit around the Earth, for the formation of tides, for natural convection by which fluid flow occurs under the influence of a density gradient, for heating the interiors of forming stars and planets to very high temperatures, and for various other phenomena observed on Earth.

Gravitation is one of the four fundamental interactions of nature, along with electromagnetism, the strong nuclear force and weak force. Modern physics describes gravitation using the general Theory of Relativity by Albert Einstein, in which it is a consequence of the curvature of space-time governing the motion of inertial objects. This means that the orbital planets, objects, are in perfect balance. A gravity pot-hole, if you will, of gravity and electromagnetism.

Electromagnetic Spectrum, Gravity and Balance

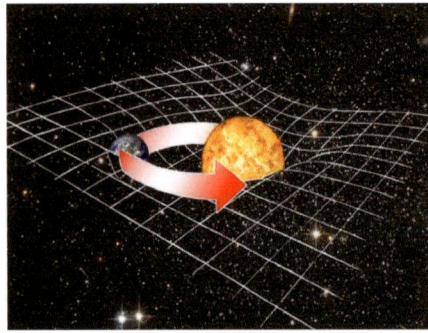

The Sun and Orbiting Earth

Relativity

Gravitation has a strong foot hold in the universe and early stages of explanation exist, but are just theories and not solid fact. We can of course explain the effects of gravity on the human body, which translates as balance.

Balance

Many indigenous tribes have practiced the art of balance for thousands of years. We see Indians using poses understood in Yoga, and Shaolin monks standing with one leg parallel to their torso for hours. Amazonians would pose as statues on tall pillars balancing on one foot for days at a time to create a sense of centring. Balance also comes in the form of dance, as movement tells not only the stories of ancient tales but of balance internally and externally of harmonious rhythmical action.

The Nervous System

We see Shaolin teachings where students are put through extreme temperature and Chi meditation. They would hit the surface of frozen water with their hands to cool their Chi as it ever increases in life force. As this technique is demonstrated, the constant cold forces the spiritual body to awaken within the heart and energise the body, to 'heat up and fight for life.' If continued for long periods of time, it can help the mind separate from the physical earthly body with further meditation.

Another technique would be to sit in a bath of ice cold water. A record breaking Dutch man, Wim Hof, demonstrates the technique found in Yoga perfectly. The Yogis call this the 'Inner Flame' which is known as the life force or Chi. It is not only this daredevil who uses the cold as separation meditation, monks and seekers of higher levels of consciousness also perform such feats.

Muscular

Holding positions for great lengths of time as well as regulating breathing patterns as by Yoga, Buddhist, Aboriginal, Christian, Muslim, Jewish, Sikh and many, many more gurus creates heat within motion. The endurance of the core exercises, chanting, singing etc., of physical endurance inflames and focuses centred mental thinking toward the pineal gland and the energetic elemental energy that is produced from within the core, the will power thus dissolving the ego' creating a divine relationship.

Another technique would be to Dance, Sing, weight lifting or even working hard in a desired loving profession etc. coupled with breathing techniques and the feeling of true unconditional love.

Chemical and Emotional

As we put our bodies through movements, stretches and contortions it produces chemicals that force our bodies to explore internally. These chemicals can be blocked within the body, not releasing or flowing in the correct natural state of balance, thereby resulting in stress, worry or unnecessary emotions. Knowing one's body mechanics changes the emotions, contribution to self-awareness which in turn makes us happy and elated with a strong focus, activating a centring into the pineal gland.

Our bodies are governed by a chemical balance which can be balanced by physical exhaustion or slight movement e.g. Tai Chi, by mental awareness e.g. knowing one's life interests, by 'identity' and by emotional energetic connection. Thus you can find belonging and understand exactly your desires.

Beauty

As we as individuals look upon beauty we realise that the beauty we interpret is only ourselves connecting with what is so unique about ourselves. The beauty is generated through you. That, or those, emotions are you feeling it as an expression.

Activity:

Every time the feeling of beauty arises in you, say to yourself: "This beauty is me that I feel". Let it enter you by accepting the moment and sharing with it.

Love

Love is the connection that bonds us in oneness. The unconditional love you have for friends, family, pets etc. is connecting you with the parts that you love about yourself. Remember, you have attracted all the things that live in your life currently.

Activity:

Meditation (see page 29, 37, 60, 81, 103) is a sure way to bring more love into your life. Actively seek a heartfelt hug every day. This could be from a family pet, pillow, God, Goddess or a tree etc. When engaged in conversations try to be more tactile. Be present in the conversation. When you experience love, say to yourself: "I am love. I see the love outwardly" and "I feel love inwardly. I am this love in this moment".

Seeing the moments that love brings, we often react internally but lessen the outer reaction through fears of self-judgment, or that of others' judgments. This conscious exercise will help bring balance and this balance will become a loving glow that all will see emanating from you.

Excitement

In quantum mechanics, an excited state of a system, such as an atom, molecule or nucleus, is any quantum state of the system that has a higher energy than the ground particles, and is indicative of the level of excitation, with the notable exception of a system that exhibits negative temperature.

It is said that atoms vibrate at a higher level if excited. So if you are not in the energies of emotions showing enthusiasm, charm, charisma or excitement your body is at ground level. This means that you are vibrating at the minimum, when you should be emitting at the most optimum in any given moment.

Activity:

Book a vacation well in advance. Try to have a spa week, alternatively a well-planned relaxing bath - the heat will increase your vibration. Meditate on the notion of a parachute jump or some adventurous activity. Make a date, etc.

Governing your correct emotions in this world of language is one piece to the puzzle.

Mental State

While emotionally meditating under the strains of submersing yourself in cold water or the endurance you feel when holding a stretch for long periods, you are constantly fighting your will power. The physical and the energetic emotions, when activated, help the mental focus in the senses of submission, acceptance and releasing to keep you within this realm while exploring the internal desires you want as a conscious reality.

Activity:

Meditate at sunrise to bring balance. This early start floods the energy body with life giving photons of colour, as life starts in the morning! As you start to use extreme ways to govern your mind by holding onto the images, *then letting go*, you seek to create your desired reality. Hold onto the warmth in every moment. If holding an enduring pose, reflect on the support that the ground, gravity the universe gives you. If submersed in ice cold water, reflect on the warmth of loved ones. Remember to build your tolerance up to increasing ice cold temperatures for extreme meditations.

All these practices of balance are a law in practice and assured ways to centre oneself and free your energy points. Stimulation is the key to working within each law and making it your own, accelerating the wheels of life.

It doesn't matter at what age you begin; the key thing is to start.

For you to find yourself is the truest legacy to leave, and as you do this it paves the way for others to follow in your frequency footprints.

The Universe at Large

Our Solar System is just one member of a vast Milky Way galaxy, with 200 to 400 billion stars, but how many galaxies are there in the entire Universe? This is a difficult number to know for certain, since we can only see a fraction of the Universe, even with our most powerful instruments. The most current estimates are that there are 100 to 200 billion galaxies in the Universe, each of which has hundreds of billions of stars. A recent German supercomputer simulation put that number even higher: 500 billion. In other words, there could be a galaxy out there for every star in the Milky Way. In order to create these estimates, astronomers use a powerful telescope such as the Hubble Space Telescope to deeply study a region of the sky.

By gathering light from hundreds of hours, Hubble is able to see more deeply than any Earth-based telescope could ever hope to. Astronomers count up the number of galaxies in the cone of space that makes up the deep image, and then use this as an average for the rest of the sky. Even though they've really only observed a tiny fraction of the sky at that depth, they can estimate the rest.

Most of the galaxies in the Universe are probably tiny dwarf galaxies. For example, in our local group of galaxies there are only 3 large spiral galaxies: the Milky Way with 200 to 400 billion Suns, Andromeda, and the Triangulum Galaxy. The rest are dwarf and irregular galaxies. It is because of our understanding of the electromagnetic spectrum that we are able to have a deep insight, enabling us to construct a better template for the universe we occupy. This begs toward evidence that this planet we so rightly inhabit has its own eco-system within the universe.

This planet is not just the paths we walk down or the destinations we seek to retreat for relaxation, it is the air that we breathe, the laughter that carries along the winds, the beating heart in your chest. We, as a species, must connect to the Earth. See how the chair that holds you grounded to the surface of the planet gives you support or how the morning sun touches your skin and invokes warmth deep within your heart.

Breath

Loving Mother Earth is another key.

Activity:

Travel to a place that has no man-made light pollution and gaze into the ever expanding night sky. Understand that it is you who is experiencing the scene laid before you. Realise that the universe is you expanding into experiences greater than you have experienced before. If we are a part of the universe, and indeed we are, we can wish for the experiences we want to experience in the moment of being, by making a choice and holding it as a constant then by releasing it into the creational process with trust.

Dog-eat-Dog. Love of Equanimity

Energy

Energy - what does it mean? Energy has to be recorded as a working force in motion to be taken seriously within the Western world. Let's say we ask a ghost to move an object. As soon as the apparition has moved the object, it is classed as a work in motion so therefore it exists.

Energy, at the emotional level, very much exists because when we feel compelled by motivational emotion, we get a burst of energy. This in turn is measured as a frequency and can be classed as a work in operation: Yin and Yang, or Omega and Alpha rhythms. Energy also has the characteristics of frequency in that it vibrates. Something that vibrates creates heat, something that vibrates creates light and something that vibrates creates sound. Energy is also electromagnetically charged. This means that everything, including yourself, the book or E-book that you hold is the same thing in this and all current dimensions.

Energy is a law that we can and do command. We just need to find the correct keys to understand this conscious treasure. It is another way to write 'frequency' in this universe. Emotions are scaled in frequency also. We know that when we are feeling happy our energy is high and lightened and when we are feeling sad we feel energy-less. Using the instruments of the 21st Century, we can measure frequency and the effects of how different emotional states change the very thing we are based on at a molecular level - our DNA.

Our very existence is owned by what emotional state we hold as a constant. With the aid of this technology we can soon understand the energetic emotional state to live within to create the optimum frequency, thus living in the truth by honouring our emotions. Now that we have concluded that energy is the rawest form of this universe at this current state, and that we are governed by emotional energies of our higher selves to serve within, then this must be a *feeling elemental universe* at this moment in this dimension. Transcendental consciousness expands after this understanding, and we move into knowing that a higher consciousness works through our very being.

Earth Chakras and Energy Points

Hearing about Chakras never really interested me until I found out that the real wonders of the world were indeed the Earth's Chakra points. Interestingly enough, the planet has seven main Chakras as do humans.

Geography teaches us about the continents, oceans, mountains and rivers of the world. Geology studies stone formation- the 'skeleton' of the earth. These sciences investigate the more material aspect of the planetary body.

The study of the Earth Chakras is more akin to acupuncture in that we are exploring the more subtle energy structure of the Earth. Earth Chakras are like bodily organs that are vital to the health of the planet and to all living beings dependent upon the various environments provided by the world. Each Chakra serves a different function, which is two-fold:

1. To maintain overall global health.
2. To transmit and receive energy encoded with information.

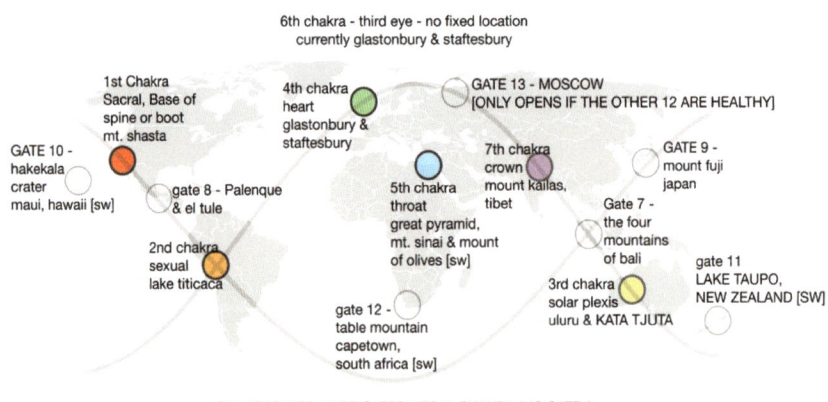

6th chakra - third eye - no fixed location currently glastonbury & staftesbury

1st Chakra Sacral, Base of spine or boot mt. shasta

GATE 10 - hakekala crater maui, hawaii [sw]

gate 8 - Palenque & el tule

2nd chakra sexual lake titicaca

4th chakra heart glastonbury & staftesbury

gate 12 - table mountain capetown, south africa [sw]

GATE 13 - MOSCOW [ONLY OPENS IF THE OTHER 12 ARE HEALTHY]

7th chakra crown mount kailas, tibet

5th chakra throat great pyramid, mt. sinai & mount of olives [sw]

3rd chakra solar plexis uluru & KATA TJUTA

GATE 9 - mount fuji japan

Gate 7 - the four mountains of bali

gate 11 LAKE TAUPO, NEW ZEALAND [SW]

CHAKRAS 1 TO 5 ARE GATES 1 TO 5: CHAKRA 7 IS GATE 6
GATES 5, 10, 11 & 12 ARE SPINNER WHEELS (SW)

The Earth has its own nervous system and arteries of circulation. Many cultures have developed systems for working with these energy lines. In Europe, research into ley lines began in England and Germany in the 1920's and 30's. The Chinese developed the art of Feng Shui. Australian Aborigines have their Song lines etc. These lines have varying lengths and widths. (Coon)

In the human body there are microscopic blood vessels and the large aorta heart artery. Equivalent on the Earth to the aorta are the two great ley arteries which encircle the planet. This, for me, was a huge piece to the puzzle.

Alpha and Omega rhythms are known as Yin and Yang energies. The following pieces of information are excerpts from Ingrid Dickenson's work on the Schumann Resonance.

The physicist and inventor Nikola Tesla was the first to carry out wireless energy experiments at Colorado Springs, USA, which produced such powerful electrical tensions that they resulted in the creation of artificial lightning. These lightning flashes also produced radio waves, that could penetrate the Earth without resistance and thereby Tesla discovered the resonant frequency of the Earth. Unfortunately, Tesla was before his time and his discoveries were not taken seriously.

It wasn't until more than half a century later in 1952, that the German physicist Professor W.O. Schumann of the Technical University of Munich, predicted that there are electromagnetic standing waves in the atmosphere, within the cavity formed by the surface of the Earth and the ionosphere. This came about by Schumann teaching his students about the physics of electricity. During a lesson about ball condensers he asked them to calculate the frequency between the inner and outer ball, meaning the Earth and ionosphere layer. They came up with a calculation of 10Hz.

This was confirmed in 1954 when measurements by Schumann and Konig detected resonance at a main frequency of 7.83 Hz. In the years following this discovery, several investigators worldwide have researched "Schumann resonance" and a number of properties and characteristics have now been established. Although the existence of the Schumann resonance is an established scientific fact, there are very few scientists who are aware of the importance of this frequency as a tuning fork for life.

At the time when Schumann published his research results in the journal 'Technische physik', Dr Ankermueller, a physician, immediately made the connection between the Schumann resonance and the Alpha rhythm of brainwaves. He found the thought of the earth having the same natural resonance as the brain very exciting and contacted Professor Schumann, who in turn asked a doctorate candidate to look into this phenomenon. This candidate was Herbert Konig who became Schumann's successor at Munich University. Konig demonstrated a correlation between Schumann Resonance and brain rhythms. He compared human EEG recordings with natural electromagnetic fields of the environment (1979) and found that the main frequency produced by Schumann oscillation is very close to the frequency of alpha rhythms.

Dr Ludwig came up with an excellent idea to take accurate measurements. When taking measurements at the earth's surface, the reading is the result of two signals, one coming from above and one from below. Subsequently taking measurements below ground makes it possible to come up with exact readings by separating the two signals.

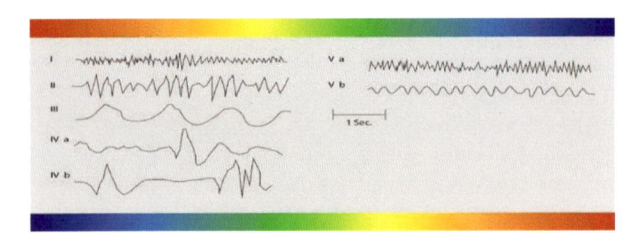

Graphs and sourced adapted from König (1979)

The graph indicated Alpha and Omega rhythms from the planet Earth and mammals. During his research, Dr Ludwig came across the ancient Chinese teachings which state that man needs two environmental signals: the Yang (masculine) signal from above, and the Yin (feminine) signal from below. This description fits the relatively strong signal of the Schumann wave surrounding our planet being Yang, and the weaker geomagnetic waves coming from below, from within the planet, being the Yin signal.

The Chinese teachings state that to achieve perfect health, both signals must be in balance. Dr Ludwig found that this is indeed the case. He wrote in his book 'Informative Medizin' that research carried out by E. Jacobi at the University of Düsseldorf showed that the one sided use of Schumann (Yang) wave simulation without the geomagnetic (Yin) signal caused serious health problems. On the other hand, the absence of Schumann waves creates a similar situation.

Professor R. Wever, from the Max Planck Institute for Behavioural Physiology in Erling-Andechs, built an underground bunker which completely screened out magnetic fields. Student volunteers lived there for four weeks in this hermetically sealed environment. Professor Wever noted that the students' circadian rhythms diverged and that they suffered emotional distress and migraine headaches. As they were young and healthy, no serious health conditions arose, which would not have been the case with older people or people with a compromised immune system. After only a brief exposure to 7.8 Hz, the very frequency that had been screened out, the volunteer's health stabilised again.

The same complaints were reported by the first astronauts and cosmonauts who, out in space, also were no longer exposed to the Schumann waves. Now modern spacecrafts are said to contain a device which simulates the Schumann waves (Dickenson, 1993-2011).

All of these theories and experiments point to the fact that the ancient teachings are correct: mankind depends on two subtle environmental signals, the Yin (Mother Earth) from below and the Yang from above (Father Sky). We can conclude that there are indeed relations between humans and the planet that we so rightly inhabit.

Clearly, the planet that we live on is a living breathing organism, such as ourselves. This made me look at perspective. I immediately regressed to a performance I had had the pleasure of being a part of. A female actress, and friend of mine, talked about the universe and perspective. My mind instantly focused on the concept of size. We can map the universe with modern technology such as the Hubble space Telescope etc. The edge of the universe, or the beginning, has the colour red (light) reducing in size. I thought of our lovely home the Milky-Way and our habitable planet Earth. Looking at our planet's life eco-systems, then cellular regeneration, breaking down in size to the beautiful world of atoms, little universes themselves, but what interested me was the basic form of everything within every dimension, which is *energy*.

All is One and One is All

Energy at its rawest form in this dimension currently has, and will continue to hold, secrets. Astrologists such as the Mayans knew that the heavens held answers to many questions. What was interesting from the Mayans' study was the understanding of electromagnetic influence over energetic elementals.

Astrology is based upon the movements and activity on each planet influenced by our own electromagnetic field, which in turn alters our energetic emotional states. We have all heard that our moods change when the full moon rears its head, no matter how far or close it touches! This is because its electromagnetic field interferes with our own electromagnetic fields, and our electromagnetic field has influence over our emotions and energies.

Studies show that our energetic emotions are indeed governed by the movements of orbiting celestial planets, which affect the electromagnetic fields within us. So, by knowing this, at times of planetary alignment or full Moon cycles, meditation, with the most innocent of intentions, helps serve to increase our electromagnetic attraction.

Vision Board

A vision board is a visual reference for creating a truly effective manifestation. We all need a plan, right?

It needs to work as a spider graph. The images need to relate to one another in harmony thus the energetic emotions and language of heart that we are going to attach in the coming chapters will be as one. This needs to be seamless so as to flow without any friction in the mind and heart.

Remember, the images you hold in your mind's eye are mostly owned by past inherited cycles and those of mass media. Now you have come to a time to challenge these parasites. It is going to be hard work but if you hold onto what you really believe and want, then you will move on with your real life.

Activity: Creating Your Vision Board

Start by selecting magazines of your choice. I personally selected home, family photos, local affairs, international affairs, car, gardens, environmental, furniture, wedding, celebrity, innovation, plane, health, holiday home, childcare, charity and design magazines. All of these magazines had a part to play in my manifestation. I carefully cut out the desired images that connected to my vision and pinned them to a cork board. Each image had to relate to a specific emotion so that, when referring to the images and the internal world, I could recall them with ease and trigger the correct response to abide by the law in each situation. This is one of the first steps to bridging your internal world with the external world. The term is known as 'mirroring'.

The universe has laws. It has neither concept of time nor good and evil, etc. It reacts to how strong you're vibrating electromagnetically and emotionally in this dimension right now. Many of us have all heard, or read about auras. Ancient artists painted halos around the heads of saints. This is your electromagnetic field, increased through acts of celibacy, innocent virtue etc. The open arms and innocent eyes are an expression of emotions; heavenly emotions. Mercy and others.

We can all understand emotions and the feeling of energies (vibes or 'atmosphere') thus we can explore the emotional world by saying "I feel so happy". The words 'I feel so happy' are a world of energetic language. By selecting the key words that relate to your images and emotions we embark upon an internal journey that has your heart at its centre. It is you that emits the information that has been selected for your vision board. It is you that will hold these within and recall them at moments when images and emotions that do not correlate with your desires arise.

People walk through life and say, "yes I would like that" but seldom receive their hearts' desires. This is because they do not have a plan. You need a plan to give you direction. You might not end up at the exact destination but you will end at the desired vision.

Welcome to Earth

Vision Board
Energetic Elemental Emotions + Images of Mind + Body of heart = Soul
Peace, Happiness, Mercy, Laughter, Wealth,
Home, Special moments, Harmonious Music,
Soul Mate, Sexual compatibility,
Social circle, Garden, equanimity.

Home & Garden

Unconditional love

Soul Mate

Special Moments

Understanding: Love:
Honouring others characters.
The knowing you have met before in another life.
Hold onto the finest details.

That special look only you and your loved one knows.
The heartfelt hug when both chests move as one.
Your song.

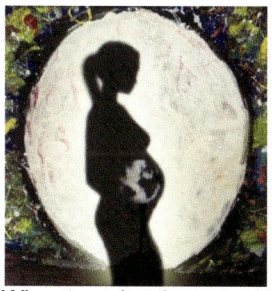

When two chest's move as one

That special look

The finest details

Heartfelt hug, love of Equanimity.

We can of course expand on these emotions and images. The key is to link them together so as to unify them all as a seamless piece of art. It is so important to use the bodily senses as these are our tools in perfect working operation.

When we start to experience the visions that first appeared as an idea within the mind's eye, we tend to let go of them. We are in the habit of saying "I have done that" and then moving on. We must remember that the holiday or the job etc. that has been experienced was only part of the overall vision. We must hold onto every part of the bigger picture to complete the frequency of appreciation or apparition.

As you connect to the vision board throughout your days, remember to use all senses as often as possible and not to use one more than the other e.g. listening and forgetting about touch, or feeling emotion and forgetting about sensing distance etc.

This conflict was very present as I travelled throughout India. I questioned why this was. The answer is that we have opposing behaviours. These behaviours surface because we have fundamentally forgotten that equanimity is a form of love! I see this as something outside of me, my 'Goddess'. Why? Because I can submit to my Goddess, and with this submission I can have compassion for all things outside of me.

This doesn't mean I am separate from external beings. It simply means that I am becoming more consciously aware of not-so-present elements already conscious in my conscious heart! It's a trigger to see the bigger picture, if you will.

This support can be present in whatever medium you find practical to you as an individual. The vision board is a beautiful mind-map that can be easily accessed through a medium of bodily movements *and we all know that movements are what form movements*!

Human Chakras

The seven main energy points that exist as our true alignment within and without the body's earthly forms are called Chakras, meaning 'Wheel of Life' in Sanskrit. The western interpretation is 'Vortex Force Centre.' Each wheel represents certain states of consciousness taking shape as energy frequencies, continuously reincarnating within the human body. They are the spirit level of the energetic body and the gateways toward the divine soul.

There is not much evidence, if any, for the existence of Chakras yet they have been around for over 4000 years. There is a possibility that they simply represent different aspects of the human condition from physical, mental and emotional, as communication for the multiple organic systems within the human body.

Each Chakra can be readily associated to the spinal cord and endocrine system, the glands in our body that regulate hormones, digestion and varying degrees of consciousness. They can also correlate to musical notes, the Base Chakra being 'C', ranging all the way up to the Crown Chakra being 'B'. This means that the Chakras are connected to the electromagnetic spectrum in terms of both light and sound and potentially the rest of the possible wavelengths.

Frequencies are produced by the endocrine system. The thymus is connected to the heart and relates to the aptly named Heart Chakra. The heart beat produces a sound wave. If the heart is under stress it beats faster, producing a different sound wave. This is all simply information exchange and representation within a system.

There are countless practitioners within the world of Chakras but we must remember, when learning about our own energy points, what energetic emotional information activates each of our own Chakra. Yes this is a basic rule with each energy point but it needs to live alongside your life story.

Human Chakras are like bodily organs that are vital to the health of the being, and to all living beings dependent upon the various environments provided by the body. Each Chakra serves a different function, which is twofold:

1. To maintain overall bodily health.
2. To transmit and receive energy encoded with information.

We are born with the tools we need to connect to our higher self. We are, in our teachings, not taught how to use them correctly.

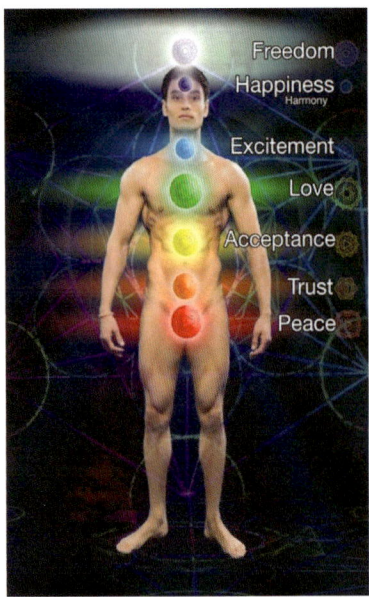

Seven Stages of Conscious Being (Chakrums)

Guided Meditation

The meditations that are programs throughout this book might need slight focus on one Chakra at a time! If not, just happily read the guided meditations present. If at any point you lose concentration, or find an image that isn't in line with your higher self, your 'vision board' look at the inside of your eyelids and banish it, (see page, 56) with the utmost compassion in your heart, then continue with your meditation.

Looking at the inside of the eyelids is hugely important as this enables you to separate the mind from the photons seen by the individual eyes, and separate the mind from the transcendental tunnelling into the pineal gland. This helps the middle way of mind work individually from the visual sense.

Activity:

Find a quiet place to sit and relax. Take your shoes off and sit with your back at an L shaped angle, with your back straight, legs crossed and fingers interlocked while placing your soft hands in your lap. This helps the alignment of energetic energy flow out of the palms of your healing hands and through you, empowering the earthly energy body.

We have many more senses than five! Remember not to rush yourself as you breathe through the nose deeply and exhale fully, repeating this a few times to start with. The breath should settle into a light, natural and conscious state before we begin.

Let's begin. Close your eyes and focus on the photons (light) that are present in front of you. Slow your thinking, separating your eyes and mind by breathing consciously in, as this is life affirming, and then exhaling consciously outward. Think to yourself, 'I am alive'. Relax your toes, stomach and jaw. With each exhalation feel the ground under you getting lighter. Feel the warmth of your skin and the support of the ground. Know that gravity travels through all dimensions!

Use your senses to hear the sounds outside of the sounds! Feel the temperature all over your body building as intensive light. Sense the distance all around your being beginning to expand, deep into the abyss beyond consciousness. Feel as though you're sitting on the edge of space, just on the edge of the creational expansion! This will help you stay connected to this earthly realm, as you explore both Internal and external worlds simultaneously to make the bridge. The Crown Chakra is the creational expansion of consciousness unfolding into conscious awareness.

Who knows what you, as an individual, will bring to this earthly realm? Feel the sense of stillness, a time of peace while continuously using the sense of distance, as you focus in-between the eyebrows (Third Eye Chakra). Focusing in-between the eyebrows stops the erratic complexity of mind shifting in and out of focus. This is where the transcendental consciousness is found, in both rhythmical silence of breath and focusing!

See your vision board in your mind rising. Focus at the eye in-between the eyebrows. See the visions that are in the vision board. They seem to be out of focus. You focus with your vision, advancing from a distance away. They start to make slight shape. Approaching, they start to come into present focus. Notice the fine details of everything, the objects that you have purchased as a fresh new life you're presently living in and sharing.

Remember to separate the feeling of 'grasping' at these things as they are already in your experience! Focus on the resolution of colour, taste, sound in the air, life in living this openness. Continuously use the language you see yourself using as your higher-self living out this dual consciousness! See the posture, and now 'walk in those shoes'. Reinforce your images with your key word or words "I have indestructible love". (See 'Love is Life' on page 65).

Now feel the emotions that you're connecting your desired visions of art, projects, and so on! Hold fast to the ever increasing resolution of colours and life that grows in this dual co-existence. Now breathe this life force slowly in, deeply focusing in-between the eyebrows as this Life enters your shared being, deep within your Sacrum Chakra.

Picture a white glow all around you like a bubble, your electromagnetic field. Be mindful that you are expanding into the feeling of distance, but still sitting on the edge of creation, safe. Say "I am alive" and breathe deeply inwards and exhale in a seamless cycle.

Stepping off the window that is the edge of creation and into your expanding life, you walk through your internal world picturing a white electromagnetic field around every object. Look with great detail, picturing the many levels of its existence, the process of how it was made and where the material originates from, the colour, molecules, atoms and the vibration you think it has. You do this by having an emotional connection to every item.

For example: my good friend bought me that glass vase and I think kindly of her. The vibration being the feeling of, 'fondness' you feel for your friend. The glass vase is a combination of sand, flint, spar, and siliceous substances with one or other of the fixed alkalis etc. This at first seems to be a lot of information but as we understand the earth we understand eco-systems thus understand ourselves. Bring the focus down into your Throat Chakra. Feel the excitement you have for something that you talk passionately about, while receiving it with equal enthusiasm.

This is still a part of your overall vision, so keep living within the internal mind's eye, in-between the eyebrows and the sense of expansion within the external realms, where every growth of light, colour and life unites. With the sense of expansion into distance, you see the colour pink. This pink-like fragrance moves playfully around as you reach out touching the enthusiastic entity. You become smitten with the colour, raising your hands over head as you spin around playfully in the fragrance of this light being. The joyful love warms your heart as it beats in your chest.

The overwhelming rhythmic feeling of your Heart Chakra opens like a beautiful flower for all to smell. With your expression of love, you share the beauty that is you, as you expand into existence. Say "I am beautiful" while feeling this shared elation of beauty. Say "I love ME" when feeling love and the notion of speaking the truth.

Breathe deeply into the Sacrum Chakra, with healing intention while focusing the breath into the centre of the forehead, where transcendental consciousness is bridged, now exhaling fully, breathing that energy of heart into existence.

Feeling the expansion of your every 'being' touching all the walls, ceiling and floor of your colourful vision, bringing your energy down into your Solar Plexus Chakra. Visualise the feeling of expansion as a white glow pushes out all around your body. Picture this pure glowing energy emanating inwardly and outwardly of your solar plexus. Picture the glow of the early morning sun. Now picture your skin having this same glow flashing on and off like a light bulb. Continuously switching on and off as this elemental grows within, increasing in speed, eventually flashes on as a beacon of pure light. The energy felt is that of acceptance. The acceptance of your desires enters you, with every breath you take. Inhaling deeply with healing intention and exhaling fully as you still keep your focus in-between the eyebrows.

Feeling the feeling of acceptance, truth and relief (honest eyes) brings you to the realisation of trust of the light works elemental beings within the universe, as you focus on the intentions of intuition and fertility within the warmth of the sacred Sacrum Chakra. Warm and elated you bring your focus slowly down into your Base Chakra.

Taking you into the wealth of possibilities that anchors within the Base Chakra, you connect to the Earth underneath you. The Earth feels light and fluttery. See your anchor! This could be the love of perception, timely walks through none judgmental nature, the pure devotion to life and the willingness to serve, the unconditional love from your husband, a business that supports your lifestyle, your children, and rhythmical music of harmonious ascensions of movements passed or unknown. Or it could be, 'my love', 'my light', 'my Goddess', 'my wife'.

It's important to know, and not to negate, the material wealth of an anchor, as these things, being stressful at times, give a lifeline, so to not send you spinning off into the endless void of endless reaches of your sub-conscious mind, when creating dimensional travel within the many layers of meditations. Remember before we reach transcendental knowing of pure truth we need to survive in the step by step process that is your true expression!

Life is, and can be, very detaching. We dissociate to find richness within lacking parts of our psyche, being bodily internal eco balances such as chemical, mental etc., and that of a more connected feeling to the divine, spiritual creational expansion of ultimate harmonic expression. The resulting transition between dissociation and re-association is the midway point that adds to the ever expanding creation that supports our children, anchors we so love as devotional life, in whatever level you so wish to express the idea!

When we re-associate, birthing appreciation in richness, becoming transcendental or not, it matters not as there are many levels of happiness, and many life-times to experience, expand and try anew! Life is indeed about richness, a tasteful variety of depth in quality gives us our unique quirks on life. Embrace these keys of musical notes of life's riches. We can mirror expression, playing alongside, or trust in 'all is well!' Your choice!

Feng Shui

Energy flowing over mountains is called a mountain dragon, and the pathway in which it flows is called a dragon vein. Where a mountain ridge dips, the mountain dragon is said to inhale, and where it rises, the mountain dragon is said to exhale.

The air around us is filled with electrically charged particles called ions. Ions are molecules that have gained or lost an electrical charge. They are created in nature as air molecules break apart due to sunlight, radiation and moving air and water. Both positive and negative ions occur naturally in the air. You may have experienced the power of negative ions when you last set foot on the beach or walked beneath a waterfall.

Negative ions are odourless, tasteless and invisible molecules that we inhale in abundance in certain environments. Think mountains, waterfalls, forests, vast pockets of water like lakes and beaches. Once they reach our bloodstream, negative ions are believed to produce biochemical reactions that increase levels of mood chemicals serotonin, help to alleviate depression, relieve stress and boost our daytime energy.

While part of the euphoria is simply being around these wondrous settings and away from the normal pressures of home and work, the air circulating in the mountains and the beach is said to contain tens of thousands of negative ions - Much more than the average home or office buildings. The action of the pounding surf creates negative ions and we also see it immediately after spring thunderstorms when people report lightening moods, says ions researcher Michael Term, PhD, of Columbia University in New York (Mann, 2002).

The University of Innsbruck in Austria rediscovered the health benefits of vacationing in the mountains. They discovered that people who holiday in moderate altitudes had lower blood pressure and pulse rates, lost weight and slept better. Generally mountain air is pure and the scenery is breath-taking (Boquetespa).

Mountains and forests (which go together normally) are charged with negative ions (the good ones) that have a positive effect thereby refreshing and rejuvenating you. A thunder and lightning storm creates a lot of extra negative ions in the atmosphere and maybe that is where the expression 'the storm cleared the air' comes from.

Generally speaking, negative ions increase the flow of oxygen to the brain, resulting in higher alertness, decreased drowsiness and more mental energy, according to Pierce J. Howard, author of The Owner's Manual for the Brain: Everyday Applications from Mind Brain Research and director of research at the Centre for Applied Cognitive Science in Charlotte, N.C. (Mann, 2002)

Free radicals (positive ions - active forms of oxygen) are highly reactive, imbalanced molecules that are the by-products of normal metabolism and are associated with the degenerative aging process. Free radicals steal electrons from healthy cells to neutralise their own charge, causing cellular damage.

Free radicals can be produced by: discharge of voltage in high-voltage networks, heating, cooling systems, TVs, radios, transmitters, radar systems, computers, exhausts, harmful chemicals and toxins. They can damage cells, cause deterioration of our physical and emotional well-being and have a role in the aging process and cancers.

Dr. Albert P. Krueger, a microbiologist and experimental pathologist at the University of California, found that an astonishingly small quantity of negative ions could kill bacteria and quickly take them out of the air so that they were less likely to infect people.

"At the University of Pennsylvania's graduate Hospital and at Northeastern and Frankford hospital in Philadelphia, Dr Kornblueh and his associates have administered negative ion treatments to hundreds of patients suffering from hay fever or bronchial asthma; of the total 63 percent have experienced partial to total relief." (health-benefit-of-water.com, 2011)

Depression is the nation's most prevalent mental problem, affecting about 15 million Americans who spend about $3 billion a year on drugs to battle it. This is not including the many other nations' that exist around the world. Almost all of these medicines target either serotonin or norepinephrine, brain chemicals which are neurotransmitters. Natural negative ions can have many health benefits, like: enhancing the immune system, increase alertness, increase work productivity and concentration, reduce susceptibility to colds and flu, relief from sinus, migrations, headaches, allergies and hay fever, increase lung capacity and stabilize alpha rhythms (a pattern of smooth, regular electrical oscillations in the human brain. These normally occur when a person is awake and relaxed. The machine used to record these waves is called an electroencephalograph, or EEG. Alpha Rhythms have a frequency of 8 to 13 hertz. Also called alpha wave) (health-benefit-of-water.com, 2011)

We also experience negative ions every time we jump into the shower or have a relaxing bath. The soothing relaxed state helps us get into the alpha state and the natural negative ions enhance the emotional frequency that we as individuals emit. When water is sprayed waves of hydrogen, 'good (negative) ions,' are released. This purifies the air around us, kills bacteria and increases our energy levels, especially in the presence of the sun.

Let us play outside as much as possible to benefit from the proximity of water and sunshine.

We have discussed many subjects on many levels within this realm, such as molecules of DNA, photons that affect our DNA and states of frequency of emotional habits that can be altered by energetic beliefs. As we become aware of the very things that we are and the levels of environments around us, we can use these natural wonders to lighten our moods and become one with them and ourselves.

Our very nature is to become aware of ourselves. As we do this our parallel universe expands into infinite possibilities. The Taj Mahal uses the tunnelling understanding of negative ions as the building is tiered from point to ground.

The Great Pyramids are also a source of great mystery with regard to their structure and they are extensively documented from 890 A.D. to the present day. You could say that they act like artificial mountains, an antenna for negative ions with numerous effects. It was found that a bowl of fresh fruit placed just feet inside the mouth of a pyramid's entrance, when compared to a second bowl placed outside of the Pyramid yielded different results. Those outside withered and rotted within days whilst those inside remained fresh for weeks to even months.

Safety razors stay sharp in a pyramid. According to scientists, microwave dehydration occurs, a dull razor blade is essentially loaded with water molecules and the dehydration simply removes the water from the steel. Coins can be cleaned in this manner also. Plants grown inside the pyramid have much greater yield. Water stays fresh. There are multiple theories: modular climates made within the structure, negative ion distribution, static torsion fields etc.

Some companies even sell pyramids with the same dimensions scaled down for the home. People use them to attain better sleep, purify the air etc.

Feng Shui within the Home and Body

Feng Shui, incorporating the discovery of Alpha rhythms coupled with negative ions known, widely understood within our extended families from overseas, brings light to stored energy and the effects on individuals.

As we understand it, human beings evolve when threatened by the environment around us, but the environment is really ourselves! Evolution isn't only massive leaps; it is humble steps toward absolution. One of the greatest incentives for getting rid of clutter externally is the understanding that keeping the objects within your environment is doing you no good internally.

There are two ways that the symbology of the many things within your home can affect you. Firstly, it is related to the negative associations you may have with something and, secondly, it is related to the frequency emitted by the object itself.

If you have objects in your home, office etc. that have unfortunate associations, it doesn't matter if they have years of serviceable life in them - they are cluttering your space and cluttering your psyche.

Another life time ago I lived and built a life with my first girlfriend. We were impulsive and full of life, choosing everything from the colour of the carpet to the lining of the bedding. Sadly, we were too young to understand the needs of each other and the love once felt, decayed. As I lived out my days I seemed to be pulled back to the parallel relationship that once was. Even years after experiencing other heartfelt relationships I still had strong emotional ties. This went on for about two years until one day I looked at my surroundings and everywhere I could see there was predecessor energy. I realised that all these objects became symbolically associated in my mind with being disappointed by women. I gradually replaced all that was. Every object replaced had the effect of 'shedding my skin'. Relief saturated my very being and the emotional tie was lost. I started flourishing in expression and attracting a much better quality of goddess's into my life!

By learning the nature of our environments, internal and external we keep our glass just so slightly empty for us to constantly receive.

Activity:

Walk through your home, office etc. and identify the energetic emotional attachments to items that surround you every day. Your mind will have images attached to these emotions. Now relate these images and emotions to your life journey to see where the emotions originated. If the images and emotions are warming then keep them all, but if they are not in line with your true self then they have no place in your future of presence.

Balance

Meditation Poses

Meditation, on the surface, is a tool to learn how to relax, thus separating you from the day's activities. Mastering this worthwhile exercise can, and will, bring you closer to a higher level of meditation. This is where we become the manifestation.

Picture your vision board, this chosen life that holds all your desires. As you activate your images and energetic emotions slowly, and with great detail, take a walk through your internal world, believing that it is indeed your real world.

I want you to imagine that you are walking past an area of your choice within your beautiful home. As you walk around you feel a pull to an area of connection, an area that draws you emotionally, physically, mentally and soulfully. Within this place, picture a vision board of what your higher character desires. As you meditate on your higher self, connecting on the ever growing relationships, we must work towards a higher meditation.

As we meditate on our higher selves, then within that meditation, meditate on your higher self's desires to invoke the manifestation. We sink deeper into the subconscious mind. This is how the universe first created itself. If we can meditate on our meditation then that meditation, meditates on that; thus infinite parallel universes are created. We have evidence that this exists in each individual on the planet, it's called your conscious mind, and your subconscious just wants to become aware of self.

I would only suggest meditating on one level before enlightening yourself to the higher levels. Meditation at the Earthly realm as well as working towards the higher self is recommended, but it is not recommended for you to leap straight into further meditation! Firstly, you will become confused and, secondly, it is dangerous as you can lose yourself in endless possibilities. You will lose sense of reality, not knowing which life is real or not. *This is why we need the Earthly Anchor.*

If a thought or feeling is a projection of your mind, then every moment 'with the lads' or living with your spouse is, in reality, you. You are spending time with yourself. This becomes exceptionally exciting when you realise the goals or weaknesses of your partner, friends, and daily activities are indeed your way of working toward unlocking and breaking the inherited cycles.

As you feel subconsciously through meditation, your conscious becomes aware of itself. We witness these types of characters that manifest our images and emotions from language of tone. The images and emotions that we hold, good or bad, take solid form as we see on a daily basis. You become aware of your internal by recognising your 'Mirrors of Illusion'.

We are told to respect our elder generation. This is because these conscious minds are the functional realities we see before our very eyes as we walk through what we experience as a daily existence. Yes, we live a life in which we have choice to direct what we see fit to suit our balance but all you see and experience has formed from the creational minds and hearts of past conscious beings.

A friend once made a passing comment saying, "How can we imagine what hasn't been imagined before?" We follow guidelines of the past to make our foundations then use the old conscious minds with our new vibrating frequency (every generation is vibrating higher than the previous) to develop or create a new. We need to know where and how the conscious mind develops in order to work toward a greater conscious mind.

We don't just look at their evolutionary gift that was given to move humanity onwards and upwards, we look at the evolutionary patterns of the conscious individual. This helps us as individuals learn how, on a conscious level, to evolve our own conscious minds and hearts.

If we attract a perfect expressional experience in the form of individuals, coincidental calls are triggered, for example, as you discuss or think about that particular person (frequency). We create parallel universes running along-side our own, desiring a need that miraculously materialises hours later, with a friend pointing you in the right direction. This is a sure way to recognise that every motion in action is generated from your lack of belief or something of full faith. We connect to stronger parts of ourselves to lead us into the unknown. We can, with real thinking of heart, pull the curtain back and look at ourselves for the first time.

As a misguided adolescent, raised on a council estate, I was surrounded by drug use as my peers were criminals and gangsters. Living in that environment, witnessing that kind of hierarchy gave light to the social programming of such people. I studied how addicts learnt to obtain their fix and how the dealers obtained their money, which was their fix. Knowing these worlds infused a conclusion - each level of these worlds had a common relationship, the ability to use the conscious mind to hold images within it to obtain the desired results.

Lying on the floor making pictures out of the thick smoke that filled the room gave light to many of the wonders. One in particular was emotions. Each event of the day gave room for growth as I experienced excitement (excitement charges the atom state). A strong will to obtain the future of the images I held in my mind as I passed estate agents, I drifted off into fantasy wishing to live in the most lavish of homes with a family that has unconditional love and a dog that has a rotating tail, constantly happy. After a while, as the memory of the smoke-filled room fades away, the life I had run from soon returns and I see the grime and the emotions that haunted me so.

Flashbacks of a childhood and the intimidating looks were interpreted by a sensitive boy with low self-esteem that had yet to be resolved. Finally, seeing friendly familiar faces, my heart filled with warmth as I once again sat in a smoke-filled room where uncontrollable laughter with conversations of the future and day's events was the atmosphere. The past, at these moments, is far, far away.

An emotional escape was the result of my past experiences. At these times, in total bliss, I compared the massive changes in mood with that of my morning to my evening. This gave me an extreme version of a field test. Emotions are a key to progress I thought to myself, and often shared my views with the charismatic people around me. For many years I enjoyed and endured life this way. Time moves rapidly with an addiction, an addiction for fantasising about the future and never achieving it.

We walk through life on a daily basis with thoughts and emotions that are not in line with us. Friends, family and strangers offload their emotional baggage onto us. This in turn gives little life to parts of your emotional cycle or cycles of bad ancestral energy.

Your universe is perfect so remember, if you are engaging in conversations of ill nature or they are continually entering your ears, then you haven't dealt with an issue correctly. This could be in the form of an ex-wife that you are still in contact with, negative associations attached to household furniture that you bought together, or frustrations or pains that you haven't forgiven or felt compassion for etc. We need to be aware of what we are holding onto mentally, emotionally and physically as clutter. Clutter has energy that looms around and appeals to bad old feelings of the past.

A client of mine, William, had a healthy outlook on life. He suddenly became aware that his parents had problems within the household and their marriage was threatening to fail. William became very stressed within his bodily temple, resulting in his grades dropping, social expression deflating and his general health was at a low. When William came to me, he was a distressed young man with problems with bullying within his institution, fear of the dark, and he had lost the ability to communicate his emotional states.

William, like a lot of us, became a victim to what his direct environmental influences played out within his days of existence. As we encounter these scenes, we may tend to feel helpless and this helplessness can make us live in a lower photon diet as the body retreats into the world of mind! This retreating into the world of mind holds no favours as you are running away from a problem that exists, which can and does transfer to the other reaches of your life!

In many popular bestsellers, the meaning of manuscripts, tapestries, paintings, etc. where God is portrayed as the infinite and the human being is portrayed as having infinite potential!

Infinite potential is the ability to know that your current conscious mind will attract information that, "DOES NOT" already exist in your awareness! This means that a progression of a thought evolves and manifests into your reality. Your reality is the observations of awareness.

Follow the Light

In the early 1980s, thanks to a sophisticated measuring device, a team of scientists demonstrated that the cells of all living beings emit photons at a rate of up to approximately 100 units per second and per square centimetre of surface area. They showed that DNA was the source of photon emission.

The photons that are stored within plant matter subsequently consumed by humans directly alter the ultra violet spectrum of our DNA.

DNA emits photons with such regularity that researchers compare the phenomenon to an 'ultra-weak laser.' A coherent source of light, like a laser, gives the sensation of bright colours, a luminescent, and an impression of holographic depth (Narby).

We have many spiritual and religious stories with the context of 'following the light'. We read and find our own connection to the chosen material. This in turn becomes unquestioned and taken as your soul purpose, or generally known as the gospel truth.

Following the light merely means letting the light in and observing when you are living in the light. For example, gaze up into the refracted blue sky, but *not the sun*. You will see many memories of great past times creating images out of the clouds that seem to be out of reach.

If you focus slightly more you will see little white flickers of light dancing all above. These are a type of photon. When opening your eyes, letting the light perception fall deeper into your body, you will notice the photon will change to a yellow, less abundant character.

This is the state to keep in. The light will naturally flood your body with positive ultra-violet light which in turn, with the correct language of emotional, intentional frequency, affects the DNA.

There are many curricula that use the understanding of light. A great example would be that of Christianity. Their ancient stained glass windows depict their hidden stories. The spectrums of light that flood the acoustically artistically built buildings force the body to ingest the photons, coupled with the specific frequencies that the metals, statues, creational scriptures etc. vibrate at. Another spiritual practice that understands the importance of dietary photons is Buddhism. Crystal and stones filter the intensity of light and heat onto the skin, in turn healing the body by affecting the nervous system and energy body. This activates emotional frequency thus reprogramming the DNA. Atoms are then excited, creating a higher vibration frequency.

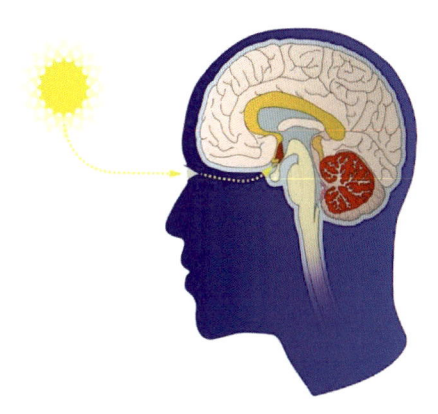

Suprachiasmatic Nucleus

At the rawest form, ultra-violet light filters deeper down, past the chemicals that bring surface joy, past the reconfiguration of DNA to the atomic state where they become excited by the higher photon state of awareness. In doing so, this increases the frequency we emit at. DMT subjects state that while in the resolution of deep perception they experience geometrical patterns that constantly unfold to higher emotions.

DMT or Dimethyltryptamine is the chemical released from the pineal gland during sleep to cause our dream state, sexual activity, childbirth, extreme circumstances, near death and death. It is vital for various conscious states, in essence every time you sleep, you get high. DMT is a product broken down via chemical and vibrational functions of tryptophan, a much needed amino acid. DMT is present in most plant life, mammals and our selves.

"Dimethyltryptamine DMT study. Subjects describe the colour as brighter, more intense and deeply saturated than those seen in normal awareness or dreams. Melatonin is exclusively made in the pineal gland, comprised of the same Tryptophan base materials as Pinoline. Melatonin induces mitosis. It does this by sending a small electrical signal up the double helix of the DNA, which instigates an 8 Hz proton signal that enables the hydrogen bond to the stair steps, to zip open, and the DNA can replicate" (Bosman 2008).

The patterns that are witnessed are that of atomic states that alter through the emotional content of the moment.

The pineal gland is activated by light, and it controls the various bio-rhythms of the body. Cold emotion leads to the enhancement of the darker EM spectrum of light rather than the warmer emotional light that resonates with our true higher vibration evolved selves.

Relate this, with real focus, to a time where you have been through a tough emotional period within your life. As you reflect back be conscious of the light that dims as you feel this way. Now reflect with real focus on a time where you felt joy, beauty, love, a happy time within your existence. Be conscious of how the light floods your very being. Remember we are governed to live within an imbalanced frequency thus one forms highs and lows.

The Great OM

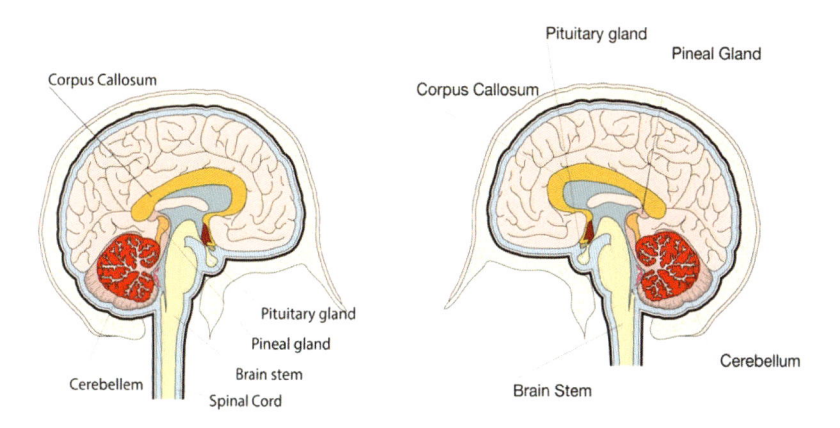

A Chant is a form of musical verse or incantation, in some ways analogous to Christian, Hindu, Jewish etc. religious recitations.

Chanting (e.g. mantra, sacred text, God or spirit, etc.) is a commonly used spiritual practice. Like prayer, chant may be a component of either personal or group practice. Diverse spiritual traditions consider chant, a route to spiritual development.

Chants exist in just about every part of the Buddhist world, from the Wats in Thailand to the Tibetan Buddhist temples in India and Tibet. Almost every Buddhist school, Christian church, Aboriginal songlines, Paganism rite and many more has some tradition of chanting associated with it.

The Great 'OM', originally from Hinduism practice, is a chant that's widely known in Buddhism and related practices of spiritual worship. It is still widely used in traditional 'Tantric' language and by many others. This is only one technique that stimulates the pituitary gland and centred hearing sense. In Sikhism there is the ONKAR. In early Vedantic literature there is the 'AUM'.

Vibrations are generated from the larynx voice box as the tongue is held in angles in the mouth with the jaw relaxed, then condensed within the nasal cavity. This stimulation evokes bodily organs within the torso! As the sound waves of the OM or other chanting sound stimulate the sphenoidal sinus wall, it acts like a tuning fork thus stimulating the pituitary gland. This stimulation carries through the corpus callosum activating the pineal gland thus bridging both hemispheres. Spiritual awareness, or symphonic unity, of a fully conscious awakening being in turn brings the cerebellum and nervous system into *body awareness*.

The different pitches produced from the larynx stimulate the pituitary gland, focusing its chemical balance within the body's emotions to create a perfect eco environment for a specific rite, incantation or musical verse! By using the functions of the body we learn just how to play the exact chord to hit the note for the desired outcome or incarnation!

The Science of Sound

If we can produce a sound at the right frequency we can shatter a glass pane into pieces. This can be seen when aircraft fly too close to cities at supersonic speed and shatter windows of buildings on the ground, or when an opera singer shatters a drinking glass with a very high note coupled with a specific pitch in the background.

Ultrasound medical equipment is used to dissolve gall stones and cardiovascular blockages, as well as for scanning foetal growth and for detecting tumours. Dolphins use ultrasound for navigation, migration and communication. Experiments show time and time again how different qualities of harmonic musical sounds affect plant growth.

Experiments with mice have also shown interesting results. The kind of music they listen to affects their brain function and growth, and also their ability to find food in a simple maze. In a study by physicist Dr. Harvey Bird and neurologist Dr. Gervasia Schreckenberg, three separate groups of mice were subjected to music by Strauss (Waltz), Voodoo music and the other to silence. Those that were subjected to Voodoo music had difficulty and became lost in the maze, whilst the others found their food with minimal effort. The neuronal dendrites in the 'Voodoo mice' did not connect but instead they were just simply wildly branching. Chaos had bred more chaos.

So we not only need to be wary of what music we listen to but what effect it has on us at all levels. Advertisers and shop owners are aware of this. Supermarkets play very soft slow music so that you take your time around the store. Other stores play hard core rock to encourage you to make impulsive decisions and therefore create a greater influx of customers.

All forms of energy vibration affect us: electromagnetic waves such as those produced by mobile phones, Wi-Fi, radio, X-rays, photon-light rays etc. Not all forms of energy vibration are understood.

Ancient Sages claimed knowledge of manipulating sound waves through mantras. They could use them for agricultural purposes, warfare, summoning demi-Gods and ultimately controlling one's mind and heart and becoming spiritually whole.

When sound enters our ears it triggers our mind and bodies, in a cascade of ways, to form ideas, shapes, desires and memories. Sound can be used to manipulate a multitude of attitudes and behaviours.

The advertising industry, as another example, is well aware of how to use sound as a medium to influence the many, even when we are not aware that we are being manipulated.

Speeches given by influential people have the same effect. Hitler marched Germany into a second world war. Mahatma Ghandi, unarmed, defeated the British Empire. When our voice is focused with attention intention and energetic emotion, it has the power to change us and all things. Spiritually we can attain these changes by the way we speak to ourselves and how we speak to others. Using mantras, classical music or even breathing techniques can transport us into higher feelings or into different conscious states.

Dominant Brainwaves

Although the brain is always emitting brainwaves at each different frequency band, it is the dominant brainwaves at a particular time that dictate the conscious state of an individual. By using audio technology to retrain the brainwaves to become dominant in a certain band we can give an individual a powerful push into the desired conscious state. By doing this we can induce numerous physical and emotional states in an individual such as meditation, excitation, motivation, anxiety, irritation, sexual excitement, relaxation, spiritualism and more.

Specific Brainwave Frequencies

With modern technology we can not only induce certain bands of brainwaves, but we can be extremely precise and induce exact frequencies. Some very exact frequencies have been found to cause effects in the brain such as the release of neurotransmitters and hormones, e.g. Serotonin or Human Growth Hormone. All of the soundtracks were extremely precise and induced exact frequencies in the listener.

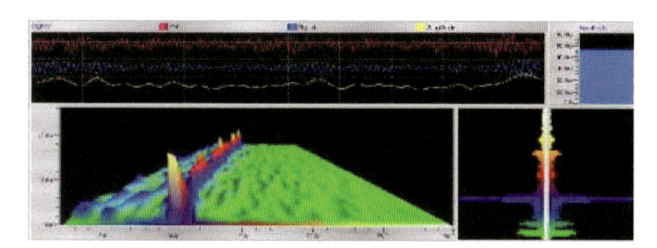

Wave	Frequency	Mental State / Sub-Categories (bands)
Lambda	100hz - 200hz	Recently reported very high frequency brainwaves. Associated with wholeness and integration. Also associated with mystical experiences and out of body experiences. Interestingly these extremely high frequency brainwaves seem to ride on a very low frequency Epsilon wave, i.e. if you were to zoom out from the high frequency Lambda wave far enough you would see that it is riding on a larger very low frequency wave.
Gamma	40hz - 100hz	Gamma brainwaves are usually very weak in normal people but have recently been found to be very strong in Tibetan monks while doing a Loving Kindness

		meditation. 40hz becomes the dominant frequency of these monks while meditating and it is also the frequency that the core of Earth resonates at. A very important frequency when it comes to higher awareness and mystical experiences.
Beta	12hz - 38hz	Beta states are the ones associated with normal waking consciousness. Low amplitude beta with multiple and varying frequencies is often associated with active, busy or anxious thinking and active concentration. It can be useful for people with ADD, depression or other emotional problems and can help with focused concentration, alertness and increasing IQ.
Alpha	8hz -12hz	Awake, but relaxed, and not processing much information. Scientists have shown that highly creative people have different brain waves from normal and non-creative people. In order to have a creative inspiration, your brain needs to be able to generate a big burst of Alpha brain waves, mostly on the left side of the brain. The brains of creative people can generate these big Alpha brain wave bursts, and do so when they are faced with problems to solve. Normal and non-creative people do not produce Alpha brainwave increases when they are faced with problems, and so they cannot come up with creative ideas and solutions. Any time you have an insight or an inspiration, you know your brain just produced more Alpha waves than usual.
Theta	3hz - 8hz	Theta waves have been identified as the gateway to learning and memory. Theta meditation increases creativity, enhances learning, reduces stress and awakens intuition as well as other extrasensory perception skills. Theta allows us to receive creative inspirations and is also responsible for many visionary and spiritual experiences. Out of body experiences can occur at Theta frequencies as can spontaneous healings and other mystical experiences. The highest amounts of Human Growth Hormone are released at a high Theta frequency and the Earths ionosphere resonates to the same rhythm. This frequency is also where much of the brains normally unused areas become most active.
Delta	0.5hz - 3hz	Delta activity is characterised by frequencies under 3 Hz and is absent in awake healthy adults, but is physiological and normal in awake children under the age of 13. Delta waves are also naturally present in stage three and four of sleep (deep sleep) but not in

		stages 1, 2, and rapid eye movement (REM) of sleep. Finally, delta rhythm can be observed in cases of brain injury and coma patients. This is also the deepest state of meditation where profound psychological healing takes place if the practitioner can enter the state while retaining consciousness.
Epsilon	< 0.5hz	Recently, the brainwaves below 0.5hz have been classified as a separate band called Epsilon. Interestingly again, we find that they are strongly related to the highest frequency brainwaves (Lambda) in that if you zoom in far enough you would see that embedded within the slow Epsilon frequency is a very fast Lambda frequency wave. The same states of consciousness are associated with both Lambda and Epsilon waves. Wholeness and integration seem to be the main themes of these brainwaves.

Brainwave Graph and Table (above) sourced from Vorly (2014)

There are even more extreme sciences within the world of sounds, especially regarding harmonic resonance. If you can meet the harmonic resonance of a structure with another source of sound waves, and manipulate those sound waves, you can manipulate the structure. Simple examples of this have already been given regarding opera singers shattering glass, and ultra sound being used to dissolve gall stones whilst still in the body. Sound frequency has the same principle as that found within the electromagnetic spectrum; the longer the wave the lower the frequency, equalling less cycles per second. Weight is inversely proportional to the speed of the wave. The bigger they are, the slower they come. The smaller they are, the faster they come.

More impressive are the experiments of Nikola Tesla, a true juggernaut of his era in most respects, especially regarding his control over electricity. What is little known about him were his experiments with resonance. He once took a simple machine that would vibrate a 15 pound weight with an 8 watt motor. His aim was to meet the frequency of the building apartment he was living in. With fine tuning he was able to make the whole building shake, much to the distress of the landlord. He found the harmonic resonance of the building. Harmonics and high frequency manipulation have been found to have even more of a unique effect on atomic structures. If a wave can meet the exact atomic structure, i.e. the wave passes through each atom uninhibited; it can be coerced in two ways. Firstly, it can be heightened to cause diamagnetism. This forces the atoms to become closer together, restricting the spin of electrons orbiting the atom. The material then has a simultaneous north pole and south pole which can induce levitation. Secondly, it can be used to force the atoms apart, causing a phase state where a solid would act like a liquid. This can mean other solid objects can be melded into it with relative ease, or it can be simply shattered like the Opera singer example. The more complex the structure, the harder it is to induce harmonic resonance.

Linguistics

As we are incubated within the womb, we sense vibrations in the forms of stroking the stomach, 'pure intentions', focusing your attention on the belly. One vibration in particular is sound waves. We know that humming or playing specific genres of musical melody has soothing effects on the unborn child. As the infant develops and learns cognitive behaviour, it will mature learning how to associate to words and sounds during its everyday life. We interpret that some words are motivating when coupled with high emotional content, and some are disheartening with low emotional rhythmical content.

A world of language is awakened within us. Finding that language can quite literally change everything, we embark upon the emotional stages of conscious mind and heart, birthing endless possibilities to situations that normally you would find stagnant. As we use language on a daily basis, and reflect on just how some words change the resolution of perception as the light that enters our bodies, we understand just how to navigate through moment to moment living.

Let's take the word 'laughter'. Try to put yourself in this state. If possible, get someone to tickle you or watch a funny film for example. Notice as you are in this emotional state of laughter how the environment is much brighter. Yes the frequency is high energetic emotion but interpreted into language is the word 'laughter'. Using your life story, by understanding that emotion plus language equals a soulful reality, the reality being the brighter perception of environment and higher energies felt.

As we walk through our daily lives most of us are unaware that our autopilots are not in the habit of processing the methodical melodies of sound that language and other immediate environmental mythical expansions bring to our versatile diet. Here are some exercises to practice to help reprogram your autopilot:

Activity:

Say to yourself once an hour, "I am alive". Breathe in deeply and repeat "I am alive". Say to yourself throughout the day, "I have indestructible determination". The, 'I' comes from the Great, "I Am", "I am able".

The 'indestructible' is the assertive word and the 'determination' is the personal quality.

Relate this to your life story. Remember that this book has the formula, but you have to use your interests of intentions, desires of wishes, etc. Whereas I had put determination, creativity, love, equanimity etc, you may already have these qualities. As we use a variety of words in the content of brighter or even darker emotions, we create an internal world. Our task is to maintain the language of heart, to emit the correct 'song of emotions' for the desired results. We know now, with the technology that the twenty first century has to offer, that we are born with two basic emotions: love and fear. There are many attachments, or grasping of each of these emotional states, such as happiness, expectation, joy, bliss and also that of hate, sorrow, jealousy and greed, but these are all attachments to the alpha states, 'Love and Fear'.

Fear is suffering in the erratic mind. The by-product of suffering in the mind is compassion in the heart, or the alpha state 'Love.' When conflict in the mind arises, invoke a 'Mother Teresa' compassion for all things in the heart.

Find, as you read these words how they also have stories attached to them. We can measure them because they are frequencies, Love having a higher frequency and Fear having a lesser frequency. So we are talking about emotions at a frequency level. The love emotion is 100 times stronger than the fear emotion. So, knowing this basic information, we can use language to eradicate the fear that draws us to that paradigm of existence. When you find yourself subdued by memories of bad content or current worries about the future, these states categorise as fears, but by replacing that filtering process with a higher emotion (higher frequency) which would be at the alpha state, 'Love' you can relinquish all that is bad.

Live in the Light

People who have been lucky enough to observe 'love' have learnt the magic tricks to life; using these laws for their bidding. We use them every day on a miniscule scale and of course on a much larger scale.

Activity:

Locate a tranquil place where you feel the soft light of life! Know that all is well in life. Picture yourself being in a relaxed, carefree state where little birds and deers come to sit by you, intrigued by how calm and open you are.

Be with all, in the best of intentions. Feel this within your belly, warmth in your belly, *expanding* forever growing forever into warmth. Then ask the universe for your wish.

Accept this. Now by letting it go of all limitations of ideology, dreams or wishing, feel welcome in your skin, heart, breath, planet and equanimity.

Mythical Metamorphosis

Originally, the Chinese traded silk internally within the empire. Caravans within the empire would carry silk to the western edges of the region. Chan Ch'ien, the first known Chinese traveller to make contact with Central Asia, later came up with the idea to expand the silk trade to include these lesser tribes and forge alliances with these Central Asian nomads. Because of this idea, the 'Silk Road' was born. The route grew with the rise of the Roman Empire because the Chinese initially gave silk to the Roman-Asian government as gifts.

The 7000-mile route spanned China, Central Asia and Northern India including the Parthian and Roman Empires. It connected the Yellow River Valley to the Mediterranean Sea and passed through the Chinese cities of Kansu and Sinking, and present-day countries Iran, Iraq and Syria. In fact Buddhism spread from India to China because of trade along the Silk Road, similar to the way Islam spread Trans Saharan Routes in medieval West Africa.

Religious beliefs of the people of the Silk Road changed radically over time and were largely due to the effects of travel and trade on the Silk Road itself. For over two thousand years the Silk Road was a network of roads for the travel and dissemination of religious beliefs across Eurasia, which is a combination of Europe of Asia, constituting 36% of the Earths land and 70% of the Earth's population.

The religious beliefs of people along the Silk Road at the beginning of the 1st century BCE (Before Jesus Christ – Before Christian Era) were very different from what they would later become. When China defeated the nomadic Xiongnu confederation and pushed Chinese military control northwest as far as the Tarim Basin (in the 2nd century BCE), Buddhism was known in Central Asia but was not yet widespread in China, nor had it reached elsewhere in East Asia. Christianity was still more than a century in the future. Daoism, as a fully developed religion would not appear in China for another three centuries. Islam would be more than seven centuries in the future.

The people of the Silk Road, in its early decades, followed many different religions.

In the Middle East, many people worshipped the Gods and Goddesses of the Greco-Roman Pagan pantheon. Others were followers of the old religions of Egypt, especially the cult of Isis and Osiris. Jewish merchants and other settlers had spread beyond the borders of the ancient kingdoms of Israel and Judea and had established their own places of worship in towns and cities throughout the region.

Elsewhere in the Middle East, and especially in Persia and Central Asia, many people were of Zoroastrianism, a religion founded by the Persian sage Zoroaster in the 6th century BCE. Based upon the struggle between good and evil, light and darkness; its use of fire as the symbol of the purifying power of good was probably borrowed from the Brahmanic religion of ancient India.

By the 1st century BCE, most people in large converted from Greco-Roman paganism to Buddhism, a religion that would soon use the Silk Road to spread far and wide. In India, on side routes of the Silk Road that crossed the passes to the Indus Valley and beyond, the older religion of Brahmanism had given way to Hinduism and Buddhism.

China itself had no official state cult of Confucius, no Buddhism, and no organised religious Daoism. The beliefs of Korea and Japan at that early period are largely lost in an unrecorded past, but they appear to have been ancestors to the later Japanese religion of Shinto, a polytheistic belief system that emphasises worship of local Gods and Goddesses, the importance of ritual purity and rule by a king of divine descent.

Religious beliefs are often one of the most important and deeply held aspects of personal identity, and people are reluctant to go where they cannot practice their faith. Traders who used the Silk Road regularly built shrines and temples of their own faiths wherever they went, in order to maintain their own beliefs and practice of worship while they were far from home. Missionaries of many faiths accompanied caravans on the Silk Road, consciously trying to expand the reach of their own religious persuasion and make converts to their faith.

The dynamics of the spread of beliefs along the Silk Road involves a crucial, though seldom remarked upon, difference between two fundamental types of religions. Generally speaking, religions are either proselytizing or non-proselytizing meaning they either actively seek to recruit new members to the faith from outside the current membership group, or they do not. In the former case, ethnicity, language, colour and other physical and cultural differences are taken to be of relatively small importance compared with common humanity of all believers and the availability of the faith to all humans everywhere.

In the case of membership in a religion, it often coincides with membership in an ethnic group, so that religious participation is a birth right and not a matter of conversion. Conversion often occurs only when a person marries into the faith and in extreme cases conversion is rejected.

Examples of proselytizing faiths, those who try to convert or induce, are Zoroastrianism, Manichaeism, Buddhism, Christianity and Islam; non-proselytizing faiths include Hinduism, Judaism and Shinto. All of these were religions of the Silk Road. Some spread along the trade routes to extend their sphere of faith enormously.

Buddhism had already spread from north eastern India into the lands that are now Pakistan and Afghanistan by the 1st century BCE. Buddhism also interacted in China with religious Daoism, especially from the 3rd century CE. Daoism, in the form of several competing sects, absorbed many of the local religious temples and doctrines of ancient China.

Christianity thrived especially at the expense of classical paganism. In Christianity's original homeland, Judaism remained the dominant but non-proselytizing religion even as it also evolved new traditions of study and practice.

Christianity spread across the breadth of the continent. The Christianity of the Silk Road was primarily the form known as Nestorians, after the teachings of Nestorius, a 5th century patriarch of Constantinople who soon outraged the Roman and Byzantine worlds with his unorthodox doctrines, such as taking from the Virgin her title "Mother of God" Nestorian Christianity spread to Persia, India and China, bringing with it the Syriac language and spirit.

The full diversity of Muslim traditions, school of thought and civilisation influences have flourished along the Silk Road. These include the development of philosophy and science, law and history, literature and arts and the expression in music and dance of the devotional and creative spirit of Islam.

The Silk Road was clearly a trailblazing opportunity for trade, either being tapestry with the story of kings, clothing made from various animals, artistic geometrical carvings, or for religious artifacts. The trade function mathematically equates the worth of information in the form of chants, light, heat and different objects (gold, precious stones etc) to create a different emitting vibration through the teachings of new, easier to ingest information in humans, being that of positive emotional content or that of negative emotional content.

What is clear to see, if using the observer's point of view, is that beliefs were, over a period of time, manipulated and transformed.

There was nothing wrong with these people that so happened to change their spiritual religious beliefs. All they were doing was re-entering information into their Chakras. As we work towards the light we can of course lose the once existing energy that flowed into our lives through the power that a formula, religious or not, has to offer.

When we start anew, we use the word 'excitement' in this example. This brings forth new energy to create the light works we need to change our focus. The power of their own creation, that people once felt through a formula or formulas that religion or spiritual worship has to offer, seldom lasts if people have no concept of focus. They may wholeheartedly throw themselves into interests but when the energy is spent they wander around lost. They may do this for years or even for a lifetime, living, hoping to feel that creational way again. The key is to change your focus. Inspired by religious 'formulas', people swiftly move faith if not aware of their changing perception of their current spiritual religious scriptures.

I found that this can be taught or observed, to breathe life back into one's self again. Relate this to your spiritual or religious stories that guide you in the worship of how to feel, act, treat individuals etc. You will find that each image of language (chant) has energetic emotions to emit and store within the bodily Chakras.

When we emit an emotion we indeed create a frequency which we live within. Focus where the energy of this affects the being! Living within a particular frequency might have guided you or helped you at a particular stage in your life. However, finding different parts (Chakras) of your current spiritual religious scriptures to find a new focus (images, language and elemental emotions), or changing spiritual or religious beliefs, helps evolve depth perception for the creation of new frequencies that are desired, for now and your vision for the future.

When a legend is born, people take notice. When a great leader dies, people take notice. When you find a burst of beautiful energy that holds you in the arms of effortlessness, you take notice. Take notice!

Emitting Emotions

To create the desired emotions to increase points of vibration, first we must activate our higher self. A diet of 70% raw organic food would assist detoxification and encourage the mind-map of this book take swifter effect at this point! This lighter consumption of energy will indeed help reach deeper into the divine vibration, that we so need to achieve to break the mould of old, undesirable consciousness! Draw back to your vision board and select the emotions that work, reassure these images and energetic emotions with the words, "I have indestructible determination" or, "I have indestructible creativity", etc.

The key words are, 'I' and, 'indestructible'. These are words that empower your vision and energetic emotions. Relate this to your vision as if it is your life story. If you are finding it hard to focus because work, or other life related images are blocking your higher-self from forming, then just say to the undesirable images or emotions, "You do not belong in my mind". Know that this is suffering in the mind, and banish it. Say "You're banished" with the utmost compassion in the heart.

Your mind should settle and your focus will return. Remember, every time an image or emotion that isn't in line with your higher self comes into focus, banish it. This could be every hour, or twenty times an hour. We are governing our own minds now, not the surrounding influences. Remember, focusing on the compassion in the heart allows you to not obsess in the dual complex mind. Do not focus on the banishing in the mind but on the compassion in the heart.

This banishing will test you at first but if you persist, after a short while the images that you feel are not in line with you will fall away and you will be left with the truth of you.

As we hold these images, and feel how we would feel when we have achieved them, we must imagine a white glow of energy around ourselves and the objects we so desire. This glow can represent an aura but realistically it is your electromagnetic field and the beginnings to using your energy elemental body.

Energy is made up of light, heat, sound and an electromagnetic attraction. If energy exists in every dimension, it can, and does, attract electromagnetically into form, through form and out of form!

The images in your mind and heart are indeed another dimension, so by holding the desired images as a constant we electromagnetically attract them together. This is known as bridging. This is your secret power. Everyday at least once an hour say, "My electromagnetic field is getting stronger".

When you find yourself worrying about work related issues or family matters say to yourself the polar opposite. If you are stressed say, "I have indestructible relief". If you can't find the rest of your story to a book that you're writing say, "I have indestructible creativity". The great 'I' and the commanding 'indestructible' is one method of reprogramming your mind. You control the amount of effort you wish to work toward, the frequency you desire to vibrate at. *Om Shanti!*

Finding myself on the southern part of the hemisphere in India, my heritage called aloud within my blood. I witnessed many of the realms living and breathing as a conscious experience travelling throughout such a place.

Rites of Passage

Carried by the demons of hell itself, I held faith as the nervous passengers gripped tight to their infantile lives. I, in tune, listened to the crazy chants and ramblings of the horseman paving a safe passage through tunnels of sound! He dared not slow his pace as we rode the dragon's back to where certain doom would be if the mountain edge so blushed our attention. These unforgiving roads had already suffered a life to the wheels of our carriage, leaving tragedy in the wake of the horseman's relentless pace.

I watched as the dread curdled in the ancient blood of these souls next to me.

With each town passed and experienced, a person's blessings and ancient teachings bestowed upon me as I accepted these awakenings!

A voice, chant, click, exhalation seemed to soften the imminent dangers that suffered the wheels of earlier towns! Did the colours, chants, religious beliefs, make all things bearable in the world of a billion plus people? A conscious wheel in the heart seemed to break the illusion I had for this nation! As no mourning saw my eyes, touched my ears of soul, from clear murder from the horseman.

Helping your Higher Self

Activity:

Stand up if sitting down, stop walking if a mobile reader. This is a technique, so apply if it works for you.

Finding yourself motionless, step backward one pace from your current location. Look at your past self as now you are indeed in the future of your parallel world. Look at your body shape and posture. Feel the emotional state of that past self.

Look at your surroundings. Think of the images that you were holding. Remember this was you a couple of minutes ago. Are you happy with what you see? Are you happy with your images and emotional state? Do you like the surroundings that you're currently settling for?

Now think of your 'vision board' higher self. Do a mental check. Imagine a house you wish to live in having a mirror. Walk past your internal mirror and see how you want to be, how you see yourself in health, wealth, luxury etc.

For far too long people put others first and forget about themselves. One day you look at yourself in a mirror and do not recognise yourself. This is because you haven't kept track of your wellbeing. This is your reality so remember to put yourself first *honourably* and then when you are full of life, *love* then give. *Heaven on Earth.*

Keep track of your health. Say at least once an hour, "I have indestructible health", but feel these states energetically and emotionally.

"I have indestructible humour, I have indestructible life." This is empowering so feel it as you work throughout your days.

As we observe ourselves with no judgment of right or wrong, we become more extroverted in the actions we seek in each conscious awakening. You will be working towards using the language that the higher self uses and the posture and grace of your higher self's movement. You observe yourself for the first time. Observe your breathing patterns and observe your body's dimensions. *Do this now.*

Don't change anything, just observe your breathing. Notice the shallowness or deepness of the breathing. There is nothing right or wrong, we are just observing our bodies in this moment. If there is any tension, observe the area of the tension. Do not try to change anything by breathing into it, *just observe*. There are no right or wrongs. Now observe yourself observing. See how you observe yourself and how you move within your living space or space that currently surrounds you. Start to walk around your space or look around your space. Observe yourself looking or moving around your space. There is no right or wrong in your actions. Observe the brightness of your space and the acceptance of your space. Observe the breathing of your body. Is it shallow or deep? Are you holding your breath or not?

We observe the thoughts of heart in a high level of energetic activity or a low level of activity, thinking as we observe ourselves. We observe ourselves some more, no right or wrong, no judgment of any kind, we are just observing. Observe if there is any stress or strains on the body. We are just observing, so don't breath into these areas, just be the witness. Observe yourself, but now as you observe yourself you are your higher self. Look as you observe your breathing. Observe that now you are indeed your higher self in the surroundings you wish. Observe yourself as you look around or move around your higher space. There is no right or wrong. You are just observing being the witness.

Observe the activity of your thoughts of heart. Are they high in activity or low? Observe the brightness in perception within your surroundings. Observe the emotions you feel as you breathe fully in and exhale out. Remember that there are no rights or wrongs, you're just observing. Continue this practice of observing yourself throughout your days. It will bring forth a frequency of energy that exists and will continue to exist if you pull it from the ether.

As a teenager, I found life a timely struggle against rebellious personalities and the competitive race toward 'gaining' whether it be social, academically, money etc! This false governing sent me into a reclusive five year period, where I found the bridge for co-existence of realm merging!

Having enough of the drug-induced formed personalities, I fell into a reclusive state!

The room I retreated into had very little light, a fold out bed that was close to the floor, a kettle for noodles and a long barbell with a 25kg weight and a walking space of 6 foot by 1 and a half foot.

This world I lived in had no walls, no ceiling, no roof and no floor of limitations!

So there I sat for five years. With eyes closed for days at a time, with my twelve hour barbell sessions and my sitting in the box splits for what seemed to be eternity, I sat, and I sat some more with no friction or concept of time

Incarnation, Magic and Imagination

Connecting to the Planet Which is You

Essentially, whatever you wish to be, your existence is currently living alongside of you! It is already you! You just have to learn to see or accept it! Meditation is a sure way of bringing 'you' into the focus. I wish for the remainder of this book to be a peaceful awakening journey for you. *My blessings.*

Activity:
Find a place that you have a connection with. This place needs to have some sound so as to activate your hearing sense: chanting, wildlife, environmental life, whatever suits! This will assist in activating your pineal gland and other crystals in the brain for centring focus.

The scene also needs to be a place where you can relax and breathe. If you can, find a river, lake or a pinecone forest for example, because the negative ions will help your mood and the air is fresher to smell, taste and breathe.

Find your spot. Take your shoes off because they restrict your feeling of touch and oneness. Sit comfortably with your legs crossed and spine straight and aligned as this helps the flow of energy project! Feel your bottom and legs become one with the Earth. Feel your Base Chakra (genitals and anus) heating up as the Earth becomes one with you.

Interlock your fingers and place them in your lap as they will keep your energy flowing and help boost your electromagnetic field. The healing hands give energy like a charge, so use them to force energy *up* through your Chakras so as not to get stuck solely in the genitals etc. Give all as energy is limitless *within and without.* Close your eyes. Relax your tongue and jaw. Separate your mind from your eyes to find clarity as you focus in-between the eyebrows. Once you have relaxed into the bodily senses, focus in-between the eyebrows, then on your hands. Your hands should be pushing energy out from the heart into your Sacrum Chakra. This activates your trust in knowing your energy is leading you to your desires of acceptance. Feel roots of energy coming from points on the bottom of your feet, legs and Base Chakra going deep into the centre of the earth. Slowly settle as you become quieter and quieter. The atmosphere and temperature around starts to activate your awareness, the sensation of your skin slowly comes alive with every breath.

Bring your focus slowly up into your Sacrum Chakra. As you start to become aware of the energy moving upward, feel more connected to the Earth that you're sitting on. Sense the trust as you feel supported by the gravity. Feel as if you are the Earth and you're sitting on stars. Focus forward trying not to look down into the void of space! A light flutters in the centre of your belly, where the feeling of fertility births. This warm sacred Sacrum of light grows inside, like the warmth of the planet herself living inside of you. Life comes from and is produced from this point in the body. We give life so we should feel connected to life. *All is one.* Inhale fully and exhale fully. Feel the circulation of the breath.

Feel the energy coming from the centre of the planet underneath you, flowing into your Base Chakra and empowering your sacred Sacrum Chakra. Use your hands to increase this energy flow. Feel the feeling of a heartfelt hug within your belly or the feeling of butterflies. Trust as you input the correct emotional information into this pure intention point within your body, with an energetic connection to all beings. Breathe in deeply and exhale fully, breathing new life into existence.

As we use the energy that comes from the centre of the planet Earth, we join our electromagnetic fields thus increasing our magnetic attraction, bringing the conscious awareness to Mother Earth. Thank her for being here! This is particularly effective if there is a full moon present. To ask the Moon and the Earth to join their magnetic fields is to honour in oneness as this invokes trust in the outer reaches of yourself!

Breathe through your nose deeply into the diaphragm as this is life assuring. Slowly bring your energy upward to connect to your Third Solar Plexus Chakra. This energy point is visible. Push this pure white energy field out of your solar plexus and surround yourself with a glowing bubble of light. This is your electromagnetic field of attraction. As you feel connected from your sacrum, increase the feeling with this glow. Using the soft healing hands, picture the desires, dreams, equanimity having this same glow of attraction. Say to yourself, "My electromagnetic field is getting stronger" once or twice to consciously activate it.

Now keep hold onto the connection through the Base Chakra (see page 28, 74) into the connection of trust of the warmth inside the sacrum and upward and outward past the electromagnetic field into your Fourth, your Heart Chakra. This is where the electromagnetic frequency is emitted. Your heart beats with the compassion felt of a new born baby. Experience the feeling of holding a loved one as they mourn a testing time in their lives. Picture a lioness standing over her cub that has fallen prey to a predator. Sit with her in that moment. Know that this is our common bond, be it human or animal alike. You are to affirm your connection of love to all around at a single time. Don't force yourself to feel your desires, just the beauty that surrounds you. Be sincere when you look into the eyes of life.

Living in the moment is holding a flower in the palm of your hand, smelling its fragrance, knowing living is seeing life in light in life. *Body awareness.*

Feel the air that touches your skin. Smell the air that clears your chest. Hear the sounds that keep you connected to this realm and help you find clarity in the deeper reaches of the inner, outer connections. As you hear the many sounds around you, know that each sound brings an enchanting story, a story of wild horses galloping through unseen lands, as cascading light bounces off the landscape, accentuating their movements throughout the rivers and mountains as they run free. Your feet washed by the passing waters of the river, you stand before the passing herd of horses. A member of the herd approaches you. With soft accepting eyes you share a moment, longing in that moment as the water whispers a magical song as the horse nuzzles at you with loving intentions. Resting her feet, she leans her head on your shoulder. Feeling a true friend has touched that light deep within your heart of hearts, she eats the flower from the palm of your hand and rejoins her herd.

The emotions that should be felt are that of receiving a heartfelt hug. This is the feeling of connection. As you feel this beautiful feeling, let it in. Let in your wants and desires and connect with your Heart Chakra, then surround it with your electromagnetic field with the image of the glowing life force of intention. I want you to imagine you are sitting in the middle of a sphere. You can sense that only the things you want to attract can enter the sphere's walls. The negativity evaporates leaving only the sound of rivers flowing, the bright colour of the sun on your skin and the smell of a fresh summers morning.

Incarnation, Magic and Imagination

Realise the feeling of connection is emanating from your heart of hearts and you are the 'Centre of your Universe'. As you feel when receiving a heartfelt hug, realise that this is the gateway to letting your desires into your solar plexus. Picture the old frequency being replaced by the new positive coloured frequencies within the sacrum as you feel your feet on the Earth's surface.

Feel as your energy starts moving up into your Throat Chakra. Start to hum. Using your voice helps you stay in this realm as we need to activate both internal and external realities to create the bridge and a solid result. Chant "Om" aloud or silently but focusing on the Sanskrit word in-between the eyebrows. By using your ears to detect sound within the centre of your brain and breathing deeply into that part also, we focus in-between the eyebrows again, allowing our mind to find clarity whist we explore our energy points further!

As you sit in your chosen place of meditation, with your tongue flat or at an angle, jaw relaxed, feel the sense of movement, the movement of expanding into the feeling dimensions of yourself. Take a moment to breathe deeply into those parts of tension or insecurities, or just feel the expansion of your being. If this makes you cry then it's okay to sit with that moment as you have found an opening into the heart.

Hear the wind blowing, rivers flowing and birds chirping outside the reaches of your body. Notice how their sincerity penetrates the different places in your skull! Listen as the softer and softer simplistic sounds of truth activate your crystal gateways of your newly forming brain patterns! Now breathe deeply into the fertility of the Sacrum and push the focus into the centre of the forehead, in-between the eyebrows. This creates a straight point of focus!

As consciousness starts to drift from the Third Eye Chakra toward the many images that flash rudely in the complex mind, focus on the sounds around you. Hear the melodies of the outer reaching birds, rivers chants etc. Hear as the sounds bring clarity. As the mind becomes tame once again, focus in-between the eyebrows to where the pineal gland is found toward the back of the skull. This place is where you'll find the transcendental consciousness, alongside the twittering birds of melodic melodies that guide you toward the truth of creation. By knowing this we then find jubilation by letting go of all knowledge out of the Crown Chakra. This feeling is that of relief, relief of expansion, relief in knowing and feeling the support of the divine heart as the universe. By letting go of all ideologies, dreams etc, we indeed let go of all limitations. This letting go of grasping at things, either being dreams, desires, identities etc, allows higher consciousness of love to enter the divine being that reincarnates within us!

The focus is to know what incarnation we so rightly want to embody, our living, breathing existence! That is a journey solely for yourself! This book is only a guide to help you see the possibilities of full potential allowed within a human body!

See that there! That is a magical door. When you entered you learnt all you will ever need to know from here on out! When you leave, you have the choice of what universe you live within. Choose well, and live a happy life. Imagination and magic are other keys.

Love is Life

You have to be willing to let people into your heart and use the love for life. Too many stories are told of love and loss. We must realise that the love we feel, whether it lasts or not, is life. After the heat of love has been lost we fall into depression, when we should instead use that particular moment in maturity, to understand ourselves. *Honour our emotions.* As we honour our emotions of clarity, we honour our ancestors. When we honour our ancestors, we become better guided as they know what is best for us, living countless lifetimes within us. *All is one and one is all.*

We have many tribal leaders that talk about ancestral spirits appearing in many forms, offering wisdom that suits the social acceptance of that particular mind-set, on that particular continent. We honour these stories because we know, subconsciously and consciously, that our building blocks of the old conscious mind *are* really ourselves reflecting on self.

These stories offer hope and the wonderful opportunity to see past all the bad that we grasp and hold with both arms, the love and life we so rightly deserve. If this book, with its content, socially connects with you, then hold on to it. Each story, told on countless continents, has a formula to guide you toward the correct frequencies of expansion toward transcendental awareness.

This heritage is part of us. Honour our Emotions:

Compassion
Forgiveness
Bliss
Peace
Mercy
Tolerance
Understanding
Love
Joy
Excitement
Gratitude
Healing
Freedom
Appreciation

We all have a measure of these qualities and emotions.

While on my global journey through finding my life manual, the people that I connected with the most, those who truly touched me with maturity etc, I would ask the most important question of: "What if one day you were to leave your children and cross over, what would you say to them?"

The scale of emotions and qualities, above all, suggests pure energetic intentions of emotions to feel, or a *safe world* of harmonies to live within! As beautiful as the answers were, and I was, and still am, touched by them all, there was a recurring pattern of rhythmic motion!

From my Journal:
Looking out of my Bolivian hotel window, I see so much construction it overwhelms the city. Is it my direct bridge from my newly forming conscious mind, telling me that my world is being reprogrammed thus my interpretation of this view that does not escape my mind? At night I seem to fall into fear as I hear unfamiliar sounds. I assert myself by saying, "I am courageous" thus the fear falls away but still this newly forming consciousness seems to be in perpetual battle with the ancient blood that runs through these veins of mine. I will not let their worlds form my own. I will fight for my existence in what is mine to command.

The constant grinding noise from the steel workers makes it apparent that I am getting somewhere. The neighbouring gramophone plays music at the most inconvenient times, reminding me of the predecessor energy that looms within my ancient blood. What a journey to be aware of! I reflected back as I had become acutely aware of these messages years previously but didn't understand or even acknowledge them. Why has it taken until the age of 29 to become aware or even to take real action?

We can sometimes do things out of character because of influences around us. Regressing and consoling with a friend or oneself, brings embarrassment, frustration, anger, acceptance then eventually we completely forget about the incidents until a pattern of similar frequencies happen again.

In many spiritual beliefs, there have been battles fought with demons, giants, dragons and many more but all are a metaphor for the undesirable frequencies that leer within our DNA. No matter how far we run, they are always with us.

Living in the mindset of not disappointing the many people that entered my life, brought forth a realisation of not being good enough as a being. This feeling stemmed from my childhood and was my deepest fear. Growing into adult life, I asserted myself as a well mannered, helpful citizen that would encourage business relations to expand, birthing freedom with wealth. As each relationship grew, the possibilities became a reality. Many conversations of lavish living filled the circles of my social activities. My life seemed to be on a high, with the beautiful ladies that I accommodated. I had time and money to waste on jet-setting around the globe and helping the people I loved. Smiles came easily from the people that I came in contact with. All of this was about to change, as at the time, I didn't realise or even recognise patterns in my life cycles.

Problems with business started to appear as tensions were high, not only with colleagues but also with my friends, as idle chit-chat came to my ears. Problems that I soon addressed and have cured since, at least I thought! Feeling abundant within myself again I found myself in Peru and Bolivia researching the energies that that continent had to offer. Upon my return I found that my life had collapsed around me in my absence. The business partners took my kindness for weakness, had fled. My women fell from my arms within weeks and my loved ones were nowhere to been seen. I was broke, on my own with not a penny to my name. How could this be? I thought, holding my head in my hands.

A time will come (and will continue to enter your life) when change is upon you. As we experience life, our emotional glass gets full with the wanted and the unwanted.

For example:

If we are engaged in conversation and a glass of wine is handed to us, assuming the drink is to our taste we take a sip. Realising that it's sour in taste we throw it away. Our bodies do exactly that. If our emotional glass is full of ignored cycles that we do not feel emotionally in line with but we continue to live out these motions, as we feel that life is tough, and so we must put a brave face on and get on with it. Sooner or later your body will tip that sour drink away.

Our energetic emotions are there to feel, so use them. If something doesn't emotionally, *rhythmically* connect with you, or it drifts away for reasons of many, and you stay with it or wait for something better before you leave it, you will take it with you to your next relationship, work life, social group, paradigm or reincarnation etc!

In each relationship I experienced in this example, I tried to hold onto something that wasn't there. These parts of my life didn't emotionally accompany my heart because their time was over, but as a forgiving species we hope and will and cry on the once was!

Knowing that the spectrum of emotions above is our true selves brings light to the breaching of foreign lands. Through the battles of the darkest of caves and the most frightening of beasts, we can live within the light as the dark was never a part of us to begin with. The actions that were out of character can be cast aside, as you know who you are now and will forever be you.

Fear is to fear itself, so if we know that fear isn't part of our true selves, then free we are. Love life is another key to healing.

Activity:

Carry a lit candle with you for one full day.
You may need two or three candles and a wind protective transparent candle container.

If the candle blows out, then light it again without fussing but if possible keep the same flame all day!

The Battle for Your Higher Self

It is easy to touch upon the positive but we, as individuals, will embark upon a journey that will test every ounce of will within us. This is because we have chosen to not settle for what we have been dealt; we have decided to change our superficial programming and seek out our true selves and not let our past, present and predestined future rule us.

I have full faith in you as the demons that you must slay will take the form of a divorce, heartache, worry etc. As your former selves will hold onto life, tooth and claw, it will feel no emotion as it is just frequency. Frequency is energy and energy exists in every dimension. As humans we put the good and bad on many subjects held as a constant. Your battle awaits with far greater reward than you comprehend. It is a time of governing for the good energetic emotions and to release the old consciousness that our ancestors formed.

Activity: Mapping the moment

Find a place where you can close your eyes and feel relaxed, where time is still and worries are nonexistent. For one hour each day record the emotions that are the foundations to the images and language you hold in each moment. As you become conscious of rising emotions, your complex mind will go on a journey, so go with it. Record as much as possible and then relate your internal world to the recurring constants in your life story. This will give you perspective on your cycles and teach you just how to break them.

If possible, document your emotional frequencies in several locations. For example, your emotional cycle in different rooms within the home, down at the supermarket, while you're in a busy setting like work, after exercise etc. Also, number the energetic levels of light (photons) that make you aware of jubilant or not so jubilant states of openness! Please try to see this as a diary and not as a table chart. Nature never moves in straight lines, only the curvature of the roots settle within the earth's crust. Be as natural as possible.

I, for example, just noticed the moment as it unfolded, visually giving it a tick if I was pleased and otherwise in the moment. So for me, there wasn't any need for cluttering my pockets with charts to carry. It is how you want to approach this exercise that makes it your choice.

This information will teach you to let go of language and live within the energetic emotional world of emitting and receiving sensations of rising and falling energies. Every moment, is quite literally governed by the energetic frequency you hold at the very root of the visual, sonic and physical world which makes up a soulful, more conscious experience.

We are governing 'oneself' now, so do not feel disheartened when looking back over the material recorded if it isn't the life that was dreamt of as a child or the years of studies at university and others proved fruitless.

The present is now, regression was then and the future is the next sentence you choose to read. To be able to be as true to oneself as possible we must look at instinct.

The Battle for Your Higher Self

When we use the word instinct what we really mean is to understand our lower, *higher* intentions and workings of the nervous system. The nervous system is our communicational electro-sensory system. As we know it every thought, feeling, motion is governed by the nervous system firing electrical emitting frequencies to generate the correct response for the moment. If the system is indeed compromised it can and does overload in the form of malfunctioning human behaviour.

Fight or Flight

Your fight or flight response is an instinct. The way we address ourselves in social interactions can trigger this basic response if feeling sociably inept. Whereas normally your character is steadfast, if the fight or flight instinct is triggered we can feel awkward, weak, shameful etc.

All of these character reactions are not your fault so do not stress about them any longer. They could be triggered where male dominance is high, where pressure is felt to put your best foot forward etc. The Fight-or-Flight response (also called the fight-or-flight-or-freeze response, hyper-arousal or the acute stress response) was first described by Walter Bradford Cannon.

His theory states that animals react to threats with a general discharge of the sympathetic nervous system, priming the animal for fighting or fleeing. This response was later recognised as the first stage of a general adaptation syndrome that regulates stress responses among vertebrates and other organisms.

In the human fight or flight response in prehistoric times, fight was manifested in aggressive, combative behaviour and flight was manifested by fleeing potentially threatening situations, such as being confronted by a predator. In current times, these responses persist, but fight and flight responses have assumed a wider range of behaviours. For example, the fight response may be manifested in angry, argumentative behaviour, and the flight response may be manifested through social withdrawal, substance abuse, and even television viewing etc.

Males and females tend to deal with stressful situations differently. Males are more likely to respond to an emergency situation with aggression (fight), while females are more likely to flee (flight), turn to others for help, or attempt to defuse the situation, i.e. 'tend and befriend'. During stressful times, a mother is especially likely to show protective responses toward her offspring and affiliate with others for shared social responses to threat.

Negative Effects of the Stress Response in Humans

The stress response halts or slows down various processes such as sexual responses and digestive systems to focus on the stressor situation and typically causes negative effects like constipation, anorexia, erectile dysfunction, difficulty urinating, and difficulty maintaining sexual arousal.

These are functions which are controlled by the Parasympathetic nervous system and therefore suppressed by sympathetic arousal.

Prolonged stress responses may result in chronic suppression of the immune system, leaving the body open to infections. However, there is a short boost to the immune system shortly after the fight or flight response has been activated. This may be due to an ancient need to fight the infections in a wound that one may have received during interaction with a predator. Coupled with the instinct are the responses of human interaction of the nervous system.

This is the inherited programming of your instinctual mind or Habit Mind. All the Habits of Mind are a collection of 16 thinking dispositions identified by Professor Art Costa. Costa defined the Habits of Mind as the dispositions skilfully and mindfully displayed by characteristically intelligent people when confronted with problems, the solutions to which are not immediately apparent. The Habits of Mind are not thinking tools; rather they are dispositions that incline one to adopt thinking tools and strategies.

The 16 Habits of mind:

Persisting – Stick to it.
Communicating with clarity and precision – Be clear.
Managing impulsivity – Take your time.
Gathering data through all senses – Use your natural pathways.
Listening with understanding and empathy – Understand others.
Creating, imagining, innovating – Try a different way.
Thinking flexibly – Look at it another way.
Responding with wonderment and awe – have fun figuring it out.
Thinking about your thinking (metacognition) – Know your knowing.
Taking responsible risks – Venture out.
Striving for accuracy and precision – Find the best possible solution.
Finding humour – laugh at the situation.
Questioning and problem posing – How do you know?
Thinking interdependently – Learning with others.
Applying past knowledge to new situations – Use what you learn.
Remain open to learning from new experiences.

Retraining the Habit Mind brings forth a new approach to our natural instinct. Whereas we might have felt cloudy while engaged in a particular moment, training the Habit Mind to instinctively answer the many subjects surrounding our apposing selves brings confidence thus a higher emotional mood equalling a higher vibration.

Looking at the many levels that make up an individual, teaches us to let go of the programming that was inherited through teachings otherwise not in line with oneself and to propel us into an informational world of whatever you want it to be. The pen is in your hand, the future is yourself and how exact you wish it to be.

Realisation

Use the word escape, as an example, instead of the word leave, as escape has at its core the word freedom. Using the word escape brings about excitement which excites the atoms within your body. When we use the word escape we will do anything to be free. When escaping, there is always a plan!

In many respects as you read this book, your mind is trying to understand the meaning or meanings of why you exist, or the reason why you exist. The reason is simple. You are born into a dual existence, both being fragmented in conflicts of decomposing and that of regeneration. 'Live this life to live.' We are born into a mind prison desperately trying to create the perfect geometrical mind-map so you can die at peace! This mind is one hundred percent dedicated in trying to control your every movement. The regeneration is those moments of geometrical clarity of conscious heart, knowing you have made the right choices so you can die in peace!

If you find this statement a little heavy remember: your journey is to become an observer, thus becoming the true creator that you are. We have all heard the saying, "You must have done something bad in your previous life." That's why a certain series of events occurred. Understanding the world around you is the awareness and the start to your life.

While travelling back from a road trip to Glastonbury with my family and friends, we stopped for a rest break at my very good friend's son's home. Approaching the home where we were going to rest our weary eyes from the constant relentless road, brought a sense of 'once-upon-a-time'. A strong familiar feeling of enlightenment awaited behind the door I subconsciously thought.

The alerting knock brought forth a man of great dimensions, not only in human appearance with a height of 6ft 6in but a massive surge of knowledge filled those slippers. Emerging from the doorway a very warm and pleasant greeting hugged my being.

Rested, we all sat in conversation around a log fire, sparks fluttering here and there, with the low light forcing deep within as our pupils widened. With the progression of the night unfolding, I found myself in a whirlwind of emotions. The similarities between us began to run deeper. I enjoyed the insights unfolding before my senses. I found myself reserved in nature while the subjects in motion became a varied sort of emotional expression in the form of martial arts, how to slow time down by using concentration, sexual preferences and reasons why characters act the way they do! Listening intensely, while giving enough to be profiled, I learnt that with expression in the many characters we are, if we even slightly ignore one of these energies that are trying to express themselves, we give that part of ourselves away. As we ignore or give parts of our true selves away, we bring trauma to oneself, resulting with the Earthly body suffering in various stages.

The night progressed in respecting the dimensions of each being, channelling of energies, 'spiritual connection', sharing of works, being honest, expressing in movement, sexual honesty, the movement in expression and the acceptance of being invited again. This assurance of my own greatness was made with a departing courteous bow.

I share this story because the events of that evening were indeed my insights. The honesty of the man, and the friend that I call him now, was in his characters throughout the evening. I connected my life and the missing dots to his tales of interest. I soon became aware that I hadn't expressed my many characters.

Expression leads to creativity, creativity leads to greatness and greatness leads you in appreciating yourself and the world around you. Expressing your creativity is key in living in the higher spectrum of elemental emotions. These motions birth unity with melody. Do not feel pressured to deny your, 'releases of creativity' in the belief that other people might criticise you. Remember, they are them and they are not you! For those people to say what is right or wrong is their interpretation of what they must do in *their* lives, they are not you. *No one else can be you.*

The biggest problem with social acceptance is that as we grow into these so called adults we let go of creation, meaning we leave fantasy in the wake of running for the next greatest thing, be it a new job, car or a big screen TV etc.

As children, we use movements, pretending to be a worm; we slither and smell the earth as we become the worm. Channelling the energy in the moment of the worm, we become the slivering, living life form that accompanies us on our mother planet Earth. If we can find each character of what we want to create in each Chakra (vortex) we can indeed express.

These traits can be seen in the visual analysis of an owner and his or her pet. I am sure you have said to yourself "that dog looks like its owner"! Another example of this is that after a time spent with your partner you start to resemble that person. I am not saying that their characters become similar because that is social grooming, but that their physical human structure becomes replicated to some extent.

That is why when you meet some people they feel like they look like cat. You say, 'Yourself might think or know some like that!' Some people feel like they are fairies, some people feel like they are wizards and some people feel like they are the expanding universe of knowledge, love and possibilities, *activating the artist within.*

To actively look at a fairy's character we see that the characteristics are what you desire in yourself. You imagine your 'being' is currently in line with your characters of being, and emit what you desire through an energetic emotional frequency (Chakras).

Every time we channel energy that results in increased mood, a series of events fall beneath our feet or *stages of conscious beings.* All of these will continue to live within your life if you *focus.*

When playing an instrument, it takes you a little time to warm up. You quickly get into the zone and expression is appreciated by your audience, meaning your energetic awakenings, but if someone talks to you or your concentration is directed elsewhere while in the moment, your flow is slightly jaded. It will take you a time to increase your zone-like expression.

When we find the levels of each zone, it can be frustrating as we have felt it before but can't live within it! This is because we have to find the zone of characters and continue to make them a habit. Once we have created the habits, we can of course resemble a fairy.

Reciprocating energies is one of the most joyous, freeing and easiest things to do.

Responding to moments of connection 'laughter' is how we feed one another's energy. This can sometimes be difficult and can leave you energy-less, as the person or persons might not know how to work toward their true higher selves. If the moment is not shared freely, in honesty, a blockage forms creating trauma to the body and soul. This illusion reinforces a lack of self-worth.

Very seldom do we let others lead us into self-discovery through their actions. The observer's world is awaiting you. We must bring all forces into existence, all of our characters as oneness, to unite the spark of creativity.

Each Energy Point Has Its Own Characters

As the development of energetic emotional frequencies form into the understanding of language, we quickly realise the coupling of motion and music of language that forms the basis of characters. We choose the particular influences that inspire the moments we so recall, and subconsciously or consciously form our own socially accepted characters.

Applying and understanding the seven stages of enlightenment that are our true alignment within the earthly body is our birth right in rhythm. Look at the many creations that surround our every day: the handle that is used to open a door, the house keys that open your home of bliss, the shower that refreshes the daily grind. We see that all of these inventions were a thought within the openings of heart and mind's eye.

These images precipitated and became solid within this earthly realm, thus receiving the benefits and comforts of their gifts. If a thought can become a solid then all thoughts, past, present or future are in fruition in our every moment, of our every day. Now relate this to a time where your character has acted out of character. I am sure you have had a time where you have sat down and thought, "Wow, why did I do that? I have never acted in that manner before".

These actions are the result of an imbalanced alignment. As we understand the language, *music of life*, that is attached to our energetic emotions, we can relate the motions to each character within the earthly primal body, transcendental body, energy rhythmic body and so on! Let's gain understanding. Before we start, know that we are merely, consciously re-entering new states into these vortexes (Chakras) with a new map ingested. We then let go so as not to *get lost* or obsess, resulting in expansion into the continuation.

Base Chakra

Love romantically, sexually, erotically. The Base Chakra has a basic formula. Mastering this helps you secure an anchor of security, thus helping you reach other expansion either being imaginary or dimensionally. The bodily senses include sexuality and sensory desire. It is okay to be spiritual and sexual!

As an attachment use the word 'peace'. The energetic frequency relates to the word peace and activates the body's beginnings of outer and inner exploration!

The genitals are connected to the nipples, taste buds, skin, distance, and other senses. Remember to let this energy circulate around the body so as not to get lost or stuck in the genitals. Relate this to your vision board. Feel where peace exists within your internal, external world. This could be your house, garden etc. Every time the feeling of peace enters you, give it to the vision as thoughts become things. When in nature using the knowledge of negative ions to increase your mood thus emitting at the optimum level so to fast track your desires.

Sacrum Chakra

Love family, children and thy neighbour. As the energy of motions rise up within you, stay connected to the planet (your anchor, your senses) into the sacred Sacrum Chakra. The Sacred Sacrum Chakra was held in the laughter of the laughing Buddha, the trust of ingestion in Mayan's and the tribal members I met while travelling throughout Bolivia.

For so long I birthed unread literature of the ways of modern human living! Being dyslexic, my world was that of landmarks and other such simplistic observations. The modern world of living I struggled with, from an early age of conscious awareness at about 4 or 5 years of age. I started to recognise rising and falling energies within people.

The contortions of the twisted faces often seek sanctuary as they came, prodding at my pop-belly. Full of heart, I could see that a pain hid out of the reach of these people, so desperately trying to figure their mind-mapping out. A heart of what they made me into, in that moment I was and still am in many respects.

Falling into the competitive race that so accompanies the city dwellers, I painfully learnt that laughter was a fight for male and female alpha states! These primal acts masked by the sophistication, contradicted one another, I thought, as an over-analysing teenager! This rebellion had a lost boy of pure heart inside of him!

Notes from My Journal:

Climbing a manmade tower that gazes, soaring over the tree tops of the Rainforest in Bolivia, I become slightly nervous as the group of tribesmen pile into this space. A swaying nervous look I must have as the winds kiss and shining sun sings their age old song. The friend I journey with beams his eyes toward me, smiling, he laughs. This laughter in turn makes all the tribesmen laugh. Louder and louder their hypnotising rhythm becomes one, hitting me like a wave of pure light. I can't help but grin from ear to ear as the contagiousness of true support becomes overwhelming. Laughing like the first time I have ever experienced such a feeling, I embrace this in the culture that is tribal living. My native friend reminds my age old blood. He said, "You see?" looking up into the heavens of the dimming night sky. "All that comes deep within (as he puts his warm hand on my belly) is support from out there in the centre of the creation. What is in, is what is out. Laughter in this place is the support of the universe". His accent carries the truth of his words, as we rejoice in the customs of his native people.

To know truth is support in the sacred Sacrum Chakra, helps the fertility grow within the maternal selves. Om... Shanti... Relate this to where you feel trust within your vision board. Reinforce the energetic frequency with your colour depth perception, as you should be more acute in the changing of perception around you. Every time you encounter these feelings, acknowledge the similarities between perceptions from the vision board and current reality surroundings of love, magic and imagination.

Solar Plexus Chakra

The Third Chakra is your electromagnetic field, this emits from your Solar Plexus. All things are essentially the same at their rawest form *energy*. We see Chakras as receiving and emitting forces, known or unknown. Some, where the origins of organs situate, serve a more skilful purpose at other ends of the EM spectrum. The solar plexus rhyme of melody is played with the attachment word 'acceptance', but this place accepts and releases simultaneously.

As a young boy I was always charged with energetic energy for running, enthusiasm to learn and move in the many kung fu films I channelled. This healthy, happy-go-lucky attitude got me off with mischievous behaviour, well *sometimes* at least! I remember a time where I would race the bus, running like the Flash out of the Marvel cartoons I so loved to watch. These moments I remember very well, because when enjoying, 'accepting' the moments we love sharing, we see what the moment brings to us! I later realised that life had, or is, a musical! If focused with the intention of *not grasping* at things, we, at different stages of maturity, allow these to move freely in and around us!

You see, when I was a young boy, full of energy, I used the interpretation of rhythmic music of life to climb trees, then would jump off into bundles of hay (the tree being the medium and the rush of air in my face being the application). These days I pretty much do the same in the words that I write.

Activity:

Picture a fuzzy, blurry white background. Within this white light, you can move freely around. Feel yourself walking forward in a steady footing as it's blurry, 'feeling around' as you would normally do in the dark, you suddenly realise that it's light! In the blurry white light you scurry around as it blinds you into clumsiness. Realising this light again, the clumsiness starts to wash off of you, as you step onto what seems to be a giant rug with geometrical patterns! These ancient symbols can't really be seen as you step again falling through the rug into water. The water is deep and blue but you feel not for the strange happenings as you see a waterfall, where a dolphin beckons, giggling as she wags her flipper-like tail. You swim closer but the force of the waterfall becomes too strong for you. The pressure drags you down into the water. Swirling and swirling around you cough, as you get pulled through a plughole, to where you float in a pinky-blue sky. A very faint soothing humming you hear, as what seems to be a cloud you're sitting on. You cutely sneeze and a bubble comes out of your nose. This bubble floats off into the distance as you watch it softly bounce, but it's not the bubble that is moving, it is you! Further and forever further away the bubble travels into the distance, bringing your focus to the absurdities of delight that you are witnessing. The cloud you feel underneath wasn't that of a cloud, but that of a Giant Otter. The cheeky fellow has a grin that tickles your eyes. Soaring high above in the world of heart, this same grin seemed to be not of the otter's but that of a hovering smiling mouth in the sky!

When cultivating levels of creativity in openness, we advance toward other observation. These observations become noticed, as more smiling people will consciously be present. These experiences that are so experienced are step-by-step states of expression toward your ultimate expression! Anything that you create as an image will indeed attract to you like a magnet! The purer the intention, the lesser the fear and the greater the level of energetic frequencies that take solid form of perception! *Like these words!*

Heart Chakra

Love all of identity. The Heart Chakra activates the healing hands and the alpha and omega rhythms within the body. This is where we infuse the omega (Mother Earth) rhythm and alpha (Father Sky) rhythm, or Ying and Yang together. The heart character can sometimes be drowned out by the imbalance of the complex mind and the confusion of where to focus, the 'mind's eye' in-between the eyebrows. This confusion brings 'grasping' at the past images of old, hurtful relationships etc, that make us choose the escapism of mind over the heart in retreat of hurt! Being honour, or heritage!

While a guest in Babylon, I encountered many interpretations that would shatter the doctrines of the preconceptions of the limited Western scientific mind! Finding oneself humbly invited into many houses, I was graced with the Goddess that each house represented! I was lost in expression as these Gods and Goddesses seemed to be emitting at a transcendental consciousness constantly. I retreated slightly into oneself.

Taking shelter in the temple and in breath, I closed my eyes to root out the reasons why, when in such conscious counterparts, I lacked expressional love!

Travelling inwardly with these observations, my being opened to a quiet part in my psyche and I found myself in a corner. This place was a dark lonely place where I curled up into a ball. I walked up to this saddened place to where I saw a flickering diamond of light dazzling on the floor. I knelt down with eyes bright as I held it in the palm of my hand. The figure curled in the corner wept. I couldn't find the other ones!

While I travelled the many planes of India, I seemed to have somehow found myself standing next to Mother Teresa's sarcophagus. Suddenly the feelings of being 'hard done by' arose within me! I was completely confused. The feeling started to take voice in my head. Shouting louder and with more cryptic controlling I stepped out of the room for a moment. Standing in the courtyard I looked up to where I see a devotee descending the stairs! She walked up to me where she looks to the problem! I mumble with no sense, *but sense is sense enough.*

With the beauty in her heart she said, "Pray for your family!" Such simple words were so impacting in the moment. You see, beings that are closer to the pure truth, birth out of awareness of consciousness and transcendental consciousness and into truth. These beings have less karma, if any, to burn, leaving them able to see more perception and feel all simplistic contortions within the truth of others! "Pray for your family", she said to me, helping me enter the conscious compassion of love for my family! Family ties are felt deeply in the psyche. To have divine compassion in the heart transcends that tie of karmic force in others.

The rising of complex erratic brain patterns can be re-guided, not just with bells, community harmonies or chants, but by redirecting the compassion in the mind! This brings peace in the mind by compassion in the heart! This in turn makes the divine bridge, birthing new, endless possibilities! Relate this to your vision board. See and feel exactly where love is touching every part, past, present and future, of your higher vision, if grasping one!

Reality is sometimes hard to live within the moment of constant state of bliss, love etc, so be patient, be kind to the regeneration of cells, and be kind to the decomposing toxins that come in the many forms!

Throat Chakra

Love your name. The great OM is but one method in activating the earthly, bodily and transcendental functions. The motion of frequency coupled with the language is 'excitement'. This state of excitement increases the electrical charge within the bodily organisms and atomic states as they resonate with other harmonious devotees, activating the pineal gland and resonating deep in the emitting torso!

This excitement can be called a heightened state of perception within the eternal world of soul! *What is in, is what is out!* We'll explain this subject in 'Sacrifice' later (see page 83). The voice box activates the ear drum thus we interpret. Not only do the sound waves connect us to the Earthly realm but to the internal realms.

Think that you can hear the sound as you hum 'OM' silently! Hear this resonant frequency of sound carrying to the focal point in-between your eyebrows. Now imagine that your character from your vision board can hear it also. This is another form of bridging your worlds. Use your bodily senses, along with breath of healing intention, to guide blood with the vibrating OM for transcendental travelling into the pineal gland.

Third Eye Chakra

Love harmonic unity of being. The Third Eye Chakra is a gateway that isn't Earthly bounded, but it is not all about drifting off into the infinite realms of soul travelling, world hopping! We can indeed have Heaven on Earth! A sure way to receive more photons into your diet would be to appreciate the night sky.

I believe that the best information we receive is not that of books, but of the never ending expansion of gazing up at the expanding stars. The mind opens to observing other stars, galaxies, etc. that filter light from other worlds into your body as you are made of photons. This in turn resonates with the reforming of the chromosomes in the DNA naturally!

Let me just bring this to your attention and reality: you will be processing and consuming photons from other Galaxies. How will these distant expressions from ingesting light, manifest in the many forms of information, relevant to the individual?

Hold onto the final picture of what is truly intended within your vision board. Hold a white electromagnetic field around each and every part of your future and present.

Remember that all the Chakra vortexes are open at this point, filled with information that you desire currently. Observe your base sense 'peace', sacrum 'trust', solar plexus 'acceptance', 'love' heart and express with 'excitement' throat of the centred images of sound you hold.

Crown Chakra

Love equanimity. As you open the Chakra gates of transcendental consciousnesses, we arrive at the Crown Chakra. Sitting on the edge of the universe, you allow the sense of new things to come! 'Relief' or 'freedom' is the attachment word. The Crown Chakra is not of this earthly realm; it is that of the never ending expanding of possibilities of perception. Think of a time when you were marvelled by a powerful sense of awe coupled with letting go of desire. If we hold onto desire (thought) then we practically live in limbo. The idea is to fill yourself to fullness then you can give!

At the age of twenty-six I made my mind up to ask my mother where my father resided. She gave me good advice and I reflected on the growing relationship my father and I had. The great thing that I hold to my chest is that of meeting my grandfather. What an amazing man he is, completely self-aware, light in his Innocent honest eyes, a very welcoming and patient, tolerant being.

While we only had a short time together he left me with a gift, a passed down secret. He said to me, "Seventy-eight years", in broken English as he only had a limited vocabulary. "Seventy-eight years", he said. "Live in the true" as he pointed at his chest.

His energy burst out of him and he was twenty again. I almost cried with the light that I felt.

I know instinctively that he had given me something that was to hold onto. "78 years", he said, as this particular feeling was shared! I gave this a lot of thought, so much thought in fact I went completely past the answer, as I do with over-thinking.

The answer is simple. Whatever makes you happy without regret and anguish is the 'true'. If you can feel as if you have no restrictions, no doubts, no lid on your container then that is the 'true'. Hold your true self in oneness.

A continuing battle is your life time. We use these many words that are coupled together to gain understanding but seldom hold them for long periods of time. If you find yourself running short on motivational energy, you need to change your focus.

Fight for a cause.
Be true to yourself.
Have something to fight for.
Love what you do.
Sacrifice physically, mentally and emotionally
Keep going.
Be faithful and Merciful.
Have a true motivation.

Activity:

Take a character from history that matches your true self. Stare into a mirror and imagine in every detail that you have their energy. Go through your energy points as you stare into the mirror. *Every great leader learnt from another great leader.*

Keep working toward a greater good.
Have an enemy and forgive yourself.
Believe that other people want a great future also.
Don't give your flesh to the unworthy.
Be willing to die.
Help the less fortunate.
Keep yourself as number one, but know that a higher being works through you!

Using different pitches played instrumentally activates crystals within the skull, dissolving the ego or selfish knowing that your action will automatically result in getting something back. Be unconditional in actions toward mapping your days of bliss. A skilled enough musician or doctor of sound can cure anything that is not limited by his or her conscious imagination. Remember that life is a game that is played with the cards of energies that blinds us with a false visual binding! Belief in magic is another key!

Sexual Meditation

Helping the flow of energy through each Chakra, we use a partner to stimulate the nerves, i.e. your skin, the senses that are your observations and the energetic elementals that bring ease of being a being. If possible, try not to: fornicate, masturbate, eat saturated fatty/oily foods, meat, sugar, alcohol or toxic mediums for a week or two (longer would of course be better to build the heightened sexual emotional energy). To eat a 70% raw organic diet would be preferred or alternatively, booking a detox retreat for the both of you. Detoxification retreats are quiet and individual journeys for you and your partner to attend together, the support of one another through these experiences would help you bond!

For these two weeks or so, symbolically, emotionally and physically stimulate your partner's senses without having the intention of anything sexual. Just let your partner know that you are there for him or her, lovingly, supportively and unconditionally. Examples would be symbolically, a picture or a statue of fertility, freshly cut flowers on the bed, a new fragrance, candles, new bed linen that are soft to the skin, fresh air and light in the home and rhythmical sexual music etc.

Emotionality gives your God or Goddess your attention when interacting as you listen and give energy to inspire new emotions. Physically be present and touch more in conversation, massage, or learn to take physical tension away. Give eye contact when interacting. Be physical without sexual motives. Gain trust with activities that ignite a closer bond! Submit in the mind and feel compassion in the heart.

Building the respect for each other's unconditional love within a relationship is key to emitting a pure intention.

We can often fall into the habit of doing something to receive and we can often fall out of the habit of appreciation. So, to rekindle appreciation we consciously work towards this treasure.

The big day of sharing the true you

The night of anticipation swirls around your heart of mind as you sit in the world that is you. With your eyes soft and glazed, the sounds around you become muffled with the quiet knowing that a night of heat and passion awaits. Your breathing is long and shallow while holding a stare into the abyss of heavenly acceptance!

Within this chapter, I wish for you and your partner to use your individual tastes on connecting creatively, energetically, emotionally, physically, mentally and spiritually in a sexual expression. Your take is unique to your expressions! The senses and emotions felt are just tools to reconfigure your states of expression towards your ultimate manifestation. During this natural sexual connection, this will heighten the expansion of the consciousness within the heart, as oneness reconnecting to the unseen love that is in constant playful expression outside of our conditioned personalities.

A base guide briefly explains a description of energy flow. The creative process is left to your individual expressions!

Your breathing starts to settle with the holding of the climax of energetic emotional information experienced moments earlier! Feeling your senses (Base Chakra 1) still tingling you focus on each Chakra point while being there for your partner. Work your way up saying, I trust (Sacrum Chakra 2) in my fertility, that my combined divine masculine and divine feminine is leading me to the destination that I desire. I accept (Solar Plexus Chakra 3) that my sense of distance, coupled with the trust is leading me to where I desire to be. I find loving beauty (Heart Chakra 4) in every moment in your eyes, as I accept and trust in my energy that guides me to my desires. I am excited to express myself in movement, sexual groans and soft talking (Throat Chakra 5) in the moment.

Feel roots to whatever body part that is touching the surface of the bed, Earth etc. See how these energies entwine in beautiful embrace. Blissfully, within the flickering candlelight you gaze upon the shoulder next to you. Slowly bringing your gaze longingly up the neck and across the jaw line of your loved one, your eyes meet, the look of love hits your heart in the moment as you inhale timely, then exhale fully sharing the moment with honest eyes (Third Eye Chakra 6). This moment of focus shared, brings the melody of realisation that everything that you could wish for is exactly in this moment right now, (Crown Chakra 7). Holding the building climax of the heightened state of creation, you visualise, sensualise, all energy as you activate your higher self, in the moment felt. In this moment of embrace, you hold tight to one another as your breath and body pulsates, building the climax, to where *relief* enters your being, as you both expand, drifting off into ecstasy.

The natural sexual meditation is a perfect way to enter new emotional energetic information within the Chakras. This might take you a couple of times to bridge into the dual co-existence of the energy body, as we can get lost in the earthly bodily senses of ourselves in the moment. I am very sure you will have fun with this sexual meditation exercise. Try to be there for your partner as you expand together.

Sacrifice

The Sacrifice was created by the observers, (Elders etc.). They understood that an action resulted in a rhythmic emotional reaction! An energetic, emotional reaction creates the melody of musical frequencies that is emitted within this feeling dimension, or universes, that you currently live and abide by! This also forces you to live within the reality you see before you. Remember, we need to live within both worlds to create the bridge. *Instinct and logic combined!*

In Greek mythology, the Labyrinth was an elaborate structure designed and built by the legendary artificer, Daedalus, for King Minos of Crete at Knossos. Its function was to hold the Minotaur, a mythical creature that was half man and half bull. Daedalus had made the Labyrinth so cunningly that he himself could barely escape it after he built it.

The Labyrinth is a singular unambiguous route to the centre reaches of your not-so-quiet psyche, quite like a maze where torment, torture and the Minotaur awaits with his unheeding thirst for control of life, consuming the very soul of our bravest.

The Labyrinth Awaits

Tales are told of a mythical beast that awaits the brave and damned throughout the walls of the Labyrinth. Silent echoes of the screams which filled the hearts that scoured throughout these impassable walls keeps you at high alert all alone in your fears. Entering this soul-less place, your movements are slowly advancing forward with the heightened awareness that brings your attention to the detailed nail marks in the cold hard stone walls interior. Your eyes widen and your hairs stand on end as you trudge through the uneven path of uncertainty, your body tense as to react to impending pain.

As the darkness of the Labyrinth shadows your every movement, you see that there is life basking within the protective armour of these walls, where no-one dares to step. A patch of bright green moss flourishes on the grey stone floor. Happy-go-lucky flies perch in the sunlight. A trail of black ants with transparent bodies as the sun shines on them use the gaps in-between the stones as pathways in which to funnel vegetation. Following the trail of ants up along the wall, you notice the blue sky and the golden glow of the midday sun. You breathe and a flood of life enters you and the Labyrinth's walls.

Empowered, you stare down the long, seemingly endless path ahead with a sense of adventure, and the knowing that within these Labyrinth walls an exit awaits. With a hop in your step you pass colourful small white and purple flowers, where the seeds must have floated in by the wind. With the sounds of birds chirping overhead, the day slowly turns to dusk. You find that the day has been long and your thighs ache with the growing feeling of exhaustion as the day has offered no food to find sustenance. Lifting your head up to gaze down the endless hall of stones, they seem to have closed in on you and the feeling of suffocation is a burden on your chest. You feel isolated and worn as you run your hand against the cold stone north wall in order to entertain yourself, your hand falls into what seems to be a wall but not! Confused in your exhaustion you stare for what seems to be a few minutes. Raising your arm, you then push against the wall, resulting in you falling to the ground. "No wall" you say to yourself quietly aloud! Shaking your head in disbelief, "What? An optical illusion had only been the first passage to my exit!" Dazed from the hours of clearly running in circles, you frantically bring yourself to your feet and touch the walls for another enhancement to the journey.

A mighty scream you express, throwing your back against the thick Labyrinth wall. While reflecting, an epiphany enters your being from the sudden emotional outburst! "If I was harboured by an optical illusion thus resulting in me being here after falling through the wall *that would be the visual sense* would it not?"

A heartfelt quietness befalls you in the hope that one of your senses will quickly find the next clue even with nothing and no one to point the way. You throw your arms to your sides and with each step your feet become heavier and heavier. By this time only the Moon and stars in the night sky bring a slight light to the endless halls of the Labyrinth.

Succumb to the stillness of the night. Your earlier fears are that of a dream, a dream of a terror that lurks within these walls. A hoot from a midnight owl focuses your nervous system with a jump at the thought that a beast lives within these walls. A cold draught touches your right shoulder, sending a judder that wobbles your head. A sigh of relief as, "It was just a draught. A draught" you say aloud. There were no draughts before, only the cold stone that accompanied my hours of walking.

You make a daring rush backward, touching each stone with passing, in the likeliest of hope that you will escape this haunted place. The efforts and time wasted journeying forty minutes backwards are felt tenfold as you crash to your knees on the stone floor. This place with its relentless unforgiving passages held no pity for the weak. A tear is felt as it makes its journey to a resting place upon the floor in front of you. The smooth shimmering surface of your tear gleams in the reflection of the night's sky.

Gazing at the collection of tears, they run in a line down the gap of the grey cold stone flooring to where you see a small spider wrapping up a fly that clearly was in the wrong place at the wrong time! A puff of air you breath out as you say, "At least I am not dead yet". The spider bundles his lunch off as you witness him climbing what seems to be a silk curtain just to the left of you. "Wow", you automatically say. At this very moment a gust of fresh air blows from the direction of the ever advancing spider. You look closely at the shimmering white silk curtain, seeing that a hive of spiders have set up camp in a crack that you just barely fit through.

Lifting your arm with no regard to the countless hours of silk woven, pushing through with the desperation of finding salvation, you barely notice the spiders that scurry on your skin and clothing. The veil of silk concealed a small tunnel, which you find knee deep in water, the sounds of the water splashing up the darkened walls and the sludge slows your movements which brings a smell of foul, choking your lungs as you gasp for air, sending you bouncing into each wall.

Turning what seems to be a corner, but disorientated from the darkness and smell, you find yourself in the sounds of waterfalls and fountains. Blissful music plays as you emerge from a green curtain that a willow tree provides. Hearing friendly familiar warm voices you fight up the slippery bank of flowing water but, weakened, you fall into the waters below. Submerged, you scramble out of the water past the slippery banks to where friends and family are awaiting your appearance. A shower awaits and good company is your evening.

These progressions of energetic emotions are a constant in spiritual religious practices worldwide, a heightened state of awareness. This can be explained in the presence of fatigue, extreme pain, high levels of embarrassment, danger or sexual arousal, overload of excitement, extreme happiness etc. At these alpha states, *Love and Fear*, we are reformed by our sense of mortality, helping the transcendental creativity of appreciation to serve!

In Greek mythology, the Elders clearly understood just how to create specific emitting emotional frequencies. In ancient times, these Labyrinths were a reality for some people and their stories spread far and wide resulting in neighbouring civilisations using the technology to benefit in that time in history! Whereas my story had a happy ending, countless real life guinea-pigs where not so lucky (birthing the creation of the Coliseum etc.) in the alternative scientific research of cultivating civilisation through the medium of human sacrifices.

"Murder rates inexplicably at 40-year lows in many U.S. Cities". According to mathematics, a 1% change in the emotional frequency of a civilisation is enough to convert the rest of society to that frequency. In June – July 1993, a group of scientists led by John Hagelin conducted an experiment in which several thousand people in Washington D.C. would meditate together twice a day for almost 2 months. This was correlated with a highly significant reduction in crime in D.C.

"An unexpected drop in crime last year, with homicide rates in some major U.S. cities plunging to levels not seen in four decades, and a rise in 'peacefulness' in the nation are among the findings of the first-ever scientific demonstration project, now entering its fifth year, documenting the long-term peace-promoting effects of large group meditations on national trends in America.

The "Invincible America Assembly" was launched on July 23, 2006, at Maharishi University of Management in Fairfield, Iowa. Dr. John Hagelin, executive director of the International Centre for Invincible Defence and director of the Invincible America Assembly, predicted in advance of the start of the Assembly a significant drop in violent crime nationwide, and improved U.S. relations overseas. Dr. Hagelin's predictions have been borne out by FBI

Uniform Crime Reports and by an independent analysis of U.S. domestic and foreign policy trends (John S. Hagelin, 1993).

The actor Tom Hanks gave a speech at the graduation ceremony at Vassar College in 2005 called the "Four Percent Solution" which has precedence regarding how small differences make all the difference. Below is an excerpt from his speech. Please find it out and read the rest for yourselves.

"Not long ago I was reading about the problem of gridlock on the freeways of Southern California--the traffic jams which cripple the city, stranding millions and laying waste to time, energy, and the environment. Gridlock is as serious and as impenetrable a problem as any we face, a dilemma without cure, without solution, like everything else in the world, it seems.

Some smart folks concocted a computer simulation of gridlock to determine how many cars should be taken off the road to turn a completely jammed and stilled highway into a free-flowing one. How many cars must be removed from that commute until a twenty-mile drive takes twenty-five minutes instead of two hours? The results were startling. Four cars needed to be removed from that virtually stuck highway to free up that simulated commute... four cars out of each one hundred. Four cars per one hundred cars, four autos out of every one hundred autos, forty cars from each thousand, four hundred out of ten thousand. Four cars out of one hundred are not that many. Two cars out of every fifty--one driver out of twenty-five drivers.

Now, if this simulation is correct, it is the most dramatic definition in earthly science and human nature of how a simple choice will make a jaw-dropping difference to our world. Call it the Power of Four." (Hanks, 2005)

The conscious efforts of the people involved disrupted the current cycle in motion and reprogrammed the old conscious mindsets that fused old frequencies of emotional habits.

If we change 1% of the population, the whole population will change their conscious selves. Don't be deluded and keep this information in one-dimensional thinking. If we change 1% of the DNA of old programmed conscious energies that exist within us we change the whole population of the self, meaning we mutate the being we travel within (Plato, 1968).

Learning to govern specific emotional outcomes through the sacrifice of the physical being, were not just the workings of the Greeks, they are also the workings of many spiritual religious practices throughout the world currently.

Christianity, with the example of Jesus Christ carrying of the cross for gruelling miles to where Jesus was nailed and crucified is a prime example. This type of crucifixion was a constant in motion; countless human sacrifices were carried out in this fashion in the 1st century AD. These angles of acts, of dimensional sacrifice, are very much in a heightened motion to the current date.

Athletics was created by the Christian faith as a form of sacrifice. The endurance observed by older spiritual, religious practices brought forth the understanding of strains upon the earthly body. The tearing of muscles, such as bodybuilder's experience, the strain on the lungs and heart from long distant running etc, all are forms of sacrifice.

In religion and spirituality, a pilgrimage is a long journey, or search of great moral significance. Sometimes, it is a journey to a sacred place or shrine of importance to a person's beliefs and faith. Members of every major religion participate in pilgrimages. A person who makes such a journey is called a pilgrim.

Whilst on my own pilgrimage throughout India, I could see a transformation in the mental and elementals as they battle with the physical exhaustion. Coupled with the visualisation of experiencing the exact place of spiritual, religious worship from scripture, brings the sense of reality to the individuals I journeyed with.

This alone can, and does, mutate the DNA into a complete overall God and Goddess-like awakening, or new state of awareness. For others, the energy that emits from the Earth location, mass vibration of chanting, mass prayer as specific harmonics, imagery, energetic emotional control and language is unquestioned and, followed precisely, unlocks the awareness *or* the touching, feeling, smelling and tasting the reality of what was a story, but now experienced in their current reality, awakens them.

Holding your socially accepted scriptures as a constant within your lifetime guides your every moment and is undoubtedly limitless of power, creation and love but if not understood and not held as a constant your power goes down and empty you can feel.

Siddhartha Gautama began by seeking out renowned teachers, who taught him about the many religious philosophies of his day as well as how to meditate. But after he had learned all they had to teach, his doubts and questions remained, so he and five disciples left to find enlightenment for themselves.

The six companions attempted to find release from suffering through physical discipline, enduring pain, holding their breath, fasting nearly to starvation. Yet Siddhartha was still unsatisfied. It occurred to him that in renouncing pleasure he had grasped pleasure's opposite: pain and self-mortification. Now Siddhartha considered Middle Way between those two extremes.

He remembered an experience from his childhood, when his mind had settled into a state of deep peace. The path of liberation was through discipline of mind. He realised that instead of starvation, he needed nourishment to build up his strength for the effort. But when he accepted a bowl of rice milk from a young girl, his companions assumed he had given up the quest and abandoned him.

For enlightenment, the Buddha, Siddhartha, sat beneath a sacred fig (Ficus religiosa), known ever after as the Bodhi Tree, and settled into meditation. The work of Siddhartha's mind came to be mythologized as a great battle with Mara, a demon whose name means 'destruction' and who represents the passions that snare and delude us. Mara brought vast armies of monsters to attack Siddhartha, who sat still and untouched. Mara's most beautiful daughter tried to seduce Siddhartha, but this effort also failed. Finally, Mara claimed the seat of enlightenment rightfully belonged to him. Mara's spiritual accomplishments were greater than Siddhartha's, the demon said. Mara's monstrous soldiers cried out together, "I am his witness!" Mara challenged Siddhartha, "Who will speak for you?"

Then Siddhartha reached out his right hand to touch the earth, and the earth itself roared, "I bear you witness!" Mara disappeared and as the morning star rose in the sky, Siddhartha Gautama realised enlightenment and became a Buddha.

The Teacher, at first, the Buddha was reluctant to teach, because what he had realised could not be communicated in words. Only through discipline and clarity of mind would delusions fall away and the Great Reality could be directly experienced. Listeners without that direct experience would be stuck in conceptualisations and would surely misunderstand everything he said but compassion persuaded him to make the attempt.

Note that Buddha didn't find the level of satisfaction of conscious being until he expelled pleasures then re-entered appreciation of nourishment. All of this is to challenge the self by sacrificing, which in turn helps manifestation or rebirth as suffering reprograms the energetic emotional information we hold as a constant from tribal ritual of sacrifice.

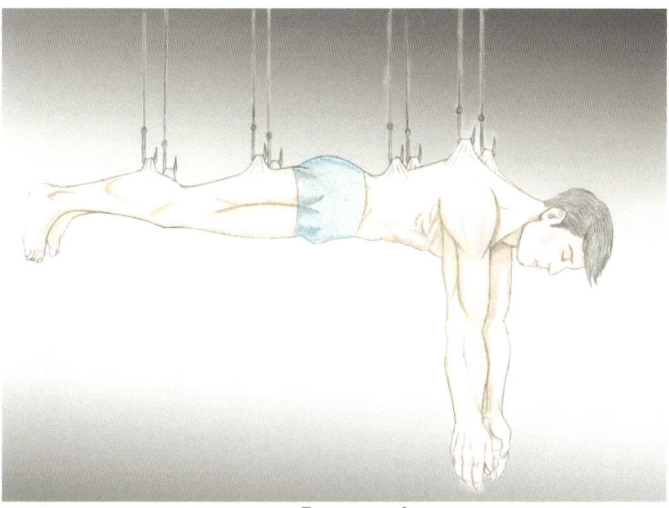

Suspension

Using physical suffering to find enlightenment comes in an array of forms. The practice known as 'suspension', hanging from meat hooks, finds its way into the bazaar world of self-sacrifice, along with monks that bend spears with their necks, practice starvation meditation for years etc!

This means we have the ability to understand our real selves and use what we really are. If we let the sadness in, we're cemented into the endless void thus passing it down through generation to generation, until it breaks with a conscious mind of a willing individual's heart. This type of emitting emotional frequency is called *'ground level'*.

Suspensions are used for meditations to gain a higher level of spiritual fulfilment or awareness to subtler symphonies. The longer the particular medium of meditation, the longer we stay within the harmonics, until one day or moment it becomes a constant consciousness, reincarnating into a Buddha philosophy or other!

The ancient precedents for this type of behaviour can be found in a variety of North American Indian tribes, or the religious practices of the Tamil of South Asia. These practices are tied to Shamanism, as the effect of the great pain and stress on the earthly body induces altered states of conscious awareness.

The Native Americans' 'Sun Dance' most often happens around the Summer Solstice. The best documented is the Sioux version, whereby dancers are pierced with wood or bone through the pectorals, with lines running to a tall pole. The dancers slowly pull, often for three or four days, until the piercings rip free. The gift of one's own body is seen as being the greatest form of sacrifice to the Gods.

The Tamils of South Asia have piercing practices as part of their worship of Murugan. Again, you honour the god with your body and offerings. The large frameworks of sharp spears, called Kavandi, which devotees used to wear, have been replaced in more modern times with hooks set into skin of the back. Pulling against ropes, the worshippers walk for multiple miles to the temple site, their suffering is an offering to the Gods along with being a sign of their devotion. Many also have a thin spike called a 'Val', symbolic of Murugan's lance, pierced through both cheeks and/or tongue for the ceremony.

The practice of sacrifice is seen in the oldest records. The archaeological record contains human and animal corpses with sacrificial marks long before any written records of the practice. Sacrifices are a common theme in most religions, though the frequency of animal and especially human sacrifice is rarely performed today! But are they? Just because we associate human physical expiring with mostly ancient practices of sacrifice, doesn't mean sacrifice isn't in full, evolved motion today.

A heightened state of sexual arousal can also be categorised as a heightened state of awareness within humans. In ancient Greece, sex orgies where practiced to ward off evil spirits and heal through the act of group acceptance. This sexual healing is seen throughout the world's scriptures but from the 5th and 6th century the popularity was controlled and became a niche market which has currently stayed in the few.

A carefully constructed sex orgy (or just you and your partner) with weeks of symbolically influencing your chosen few etc., can result in a mass of people emitting a particular emitting energetic emotional frequency. This can of course be seen today with the influences of mass media and why 'sex sells'.

Using sexual practices to open the Chakra points of energy is a very natural and effortless way of manifestation. The trouble is that most people do not use the opportunity of connecting with a sexual partner for manifestation or are even aware that it exists.

When we participate in such acts our bodies become open to the primal senses of our being. We lose ourselves in high erotic flavours and every sense, pore and nerve-ending becomes alive, this gravitational pull pulling you and your God or Goddess together as one. This oneness gives trust and acceptance, love and excitement, images and release, which are all indeed your Chakra points of energy. As you become aware of these observations, while being there for your partner, you can send your focus within the pineal gland and to each Chakra point, re-entering information that suits your desires of your current existence as a conscious being.

Remember, as we experience the very thing we created as a vision we must continue to give energy to that part of the vision to create the overall manifestation of harmonic desires.

Sacrifice isn't just a conscious progression of enlightenment; it also comes in the form of addictions such as alcohol abuse, drug abuse, social acceptance abuse and emotional abuse. We put our physical being under stresses and strains unwillingly as a form of sacrifice.

If we can learn to understand and govern the patterns of our individual physical elementals as sacrifices, we can indeed use or change the frequency *if that doesn't suit* what you are willing to create as that particular energetic angle of frequency or human being.

Kung Fu masters support the building of Qi or Chi by practicing the art of celibacy. This ancient art of celibacy was observed and taught in countless spiritual, religious forms throughout the world's scriptures. The personal development and self-discovery of celibacy practiced by Buddhism, Christianity, Hinduism and countless other spiritual beliefs reflects their commitment.

One hundred days of celibacy to build a foundation is said to build enough Qi, Chi or Prana to convert into Shen which indeed helps you on the journey of enlightenment.

Chi

Chi has been known, studied and written about for over 10,000 years. It can be found in several cultures and countries including India and South America. The most associate, alternative, scientific energy works within Japan, China and India. All these consider Chi to be the foundation of the universe that flows through all energy and life. It is the eternal balance between Yin energy, the receiving, negative and yielding forms, and Yang energy, the creating, positive and unyielding forms. Chi literally means 'life energy' and can also be known as Ki, Qi, Prana, Orgone energy.

Our ancestors developed an understanding of Chi for a better way to live in harmony with all of nature. This gave birth to many therapies used today such as: Reiki, massage (incidentally, the first type of medicine for the Western World), reflexology (which dates back to Egypt), Yoga, Kung Fu, Feng Shui and Acupressure.

Within the human body, Chi flows through pathways called meridans or dragon veins. These correspond to certain organs and limbs of the body, depending where they lay upon the body. If one of these lines were disturbed or blocked, by dis-ease, stress, drugs, for example, the body becomes out of balance and cannot perform well. With the right treatment they can be unblocked; a direct example is acupressure as it pinpoints the distress and releases it via massage or needles into or near the area.

The development of acupuncture seems to be shrouded in mystery, often how most great inventions were discovered, by accident. A Chinese soldier had a stiff painful shoulder and asked his doctor to heal him. To no avail, the doctor could not help. The soldier shrugged it off and continued his duty. During a battle the warrior took an arrow to the leg but miraculously found his shoulder had fully recovered. Returning to his doctor to be treated he told the story and the doctor was bemused. Another patient appeared with a shoulder injury and he took it upon himself to test the coincidence. So by placing an arrow head in the leg at the same place as the first patient, he cured the second and was then renowned for being the best shoulder specialist in the land.

All practices have their histories more defined and will leave them to the true historians. Chi awareness and treatments seems to appear on different continents with no communication of their individual practices, and when they do converge they are sympathetic in understanding.

In the book "The Body Electric", Thelma Moss, PhD, once a sceptic found, via two other scientists, acupuncture points present using a special device.

"Ken pulled out still another electrical device, a special meter to which was attached a narrow metal probe. He pointed out when the metal probe was not active, the meter registered zero, indicating no electrical current. Then he began to move the probe over my skin... I watched, and the needle remained at zero – until suddenly it shot way over, showing an electrical charge of some kind. Ken pulled out an acupuncture chart, and the points on the chart

seemed, generally, to correspond to the places where the deflections occurred" (Moss 1981).

There are many modern research bodies conducting MRI scans on patients receiving acupuncture. For example, the joint experiments held by the University of Maryland School of Medicine, USA and Shanghai University of Traditional Chinese Medicine, with exhaustive lists of positive results.

"Recent clinical trial and systematic review results clearly show acupuncture to be more beneficial than conventional standard care for many pain conditions...an extensive body of acupuncture research has been published, much of it with important clinical implications." (HealthCare Medicine Institute, 2012)

For over 4000 years, Ma Bo, Chi Walking and Tai Chi, have been known to cure headaches, depression, and heart disease and other illnesses western medicine cannot cure (Wang 2004).

Some cases are truly life affirming. One woman suffered from early menopause and could not conceive children. As a last effort she asked for the help of a Chinese Medicine practitioner who gladly took on her case. After three months of acupuncture her body returned to normal and shortly afterward she became pregnant with her first child.

Meditation is the simplest form of Chi cultivation. It holds the essential keys to Chi manipulation. Slow, deep rhythmic breathing, intentional movement, awareness of body and surroundings and visualisation of Chi flow being breathed in, flowing through the body as a cycle and then out, is a complete foundation to the principle of energy work. Anyone can access and achieve this and the health benefits are numerous. The more active the Chi practices, the higher the benefits.

Chi Masters are capable of some impressive feats and scientific discovery. Many can increase the heat of objects via projection from their hands, burning cloth and holes through light materials. Others can electrocute by touch, yet electronic devices cannot detect any voltage. Some imagine beams of water shooting out of their limbs into infinity as a visualisation technique so as to achieve an immoveable self and feel the flow of Chi. Kung Fu masters can pinpoint parts of the body and shut down limbs, damage the organs without bruising the skin and stop the heart.

Once the ego is gone, a Chi is able to flow uninhibited. The mind and body are the same thing. In Chinese philosophy, the mind and the heart are also the same thing; there are no divisions, only those made by men. Everything is in sway, when Yang rises to its peak it becomes Yin and vice versa. Like the Law of Conservation of Energy, nothing is destroyed, only transformed.

Breathing

Activity:

Breathing technique, take your time, trying to live the experience fully and focus. Calmly, inhale deeply at one hundred percent lung capacity and exhale fully with a clear mind. Repeat this process until instructed.

Feel as if you are on a luxury boat, your luxury boat. You are heading to an unknown, uncharted spot in the Mariana Trench in the Pacific Ocean. Enjoying your partner's company, while sipping a glass of your favourite tonic, as you approach the coordinates.

Shutting down the motor of the boat you slowly drift to a halt, which brings butterflies to your belly. The gentle wind of the ocean air touches your face and you inhale deeply. You are about to embark upon a scuba diving exploration, and you're excited to explore the unknown depths. As you enter the warm waters of the vast ocean that has no rules, no rights and no wrongs, your body starts to relax. You bid farewell as you are exploring on your own, while your partner relaxes on deck. Bring your body into awareness by using your senses. Centre yourself. Om Shanti.

Entering the water, the weightlessness of your body is felt as you swim further, forever further into the deep warm, progressing darkness of adventure. You focus on your breathing patterns as oxygen is limited. Feeling the pressure on your body as you descend, with the heat of the sun on your skin, you gracefully become one with your senses, appreciating the shimmering light that bursts through the surface of the blue ocean, creating magnificent golden portals of heavenly light that filters down from the tides above.

A sense of oneness with nature ignites within you. A smile is broad across your face as you pay homage to a Whale Shark that becomes inquisitive of the enlightened emotions you communicate with. A trail of bubbles floats to the surface as you swim upside down, bidding farewell to the spotted giant of the sea. "The thrill is afoot" you say to yourself.

On your journey through the deep blue ocean, a vast canyon appears and the sense of flying pulsates through your body. Your eyes widen and your arms extend with the beating of your heart. The canyon is monumentally enormous and a feeling of falling is felt. Your attention is swiftly altered as a trail of golden, reflecting fish usher past, gleaming in the sun's light as they cast a living shadow on the canyon's face, which draws your attention to the mouth of a cave. Little dots seemingly grow bigger and a beautiful coral reef is your scene.

The huge living eco shelf is a peaceful one with schools of grey and white hammerhead sharks overhead, Galapagos sharks with their cat-like eyes deep in thought and Manta Rays effortlessly gliding through the blue ocean. Thousands of cleaning stations where cleaner fish in their bright array of mixed colours: yellows, blues, pinks, and oranges, their dazzling movements seemingly hypnotise the predators while thoroughly exfoliating their skin.

A nurse shark scratches his chin on a smooth like surface, small dolphin pods talk and play the age old 'catch me if you can' while orange frog fish make gurgling noises as they eat the purple algae. This place, with its vast abundance of colours and life, has no sense of urgency. A great white shark, sparkling from the benefits of a nearby cleaning station, swims by, stroking your shoulder with the glance that brings warmth to your heart. Peering over to the stimulus that drew your attention, you feel a light-heartedness as you marvel at the deep and its many creatures.

Descending several meters, you breathe at fifty percent lung capacity at a cross-roads, with the passing of a whirling school of silver fish which dazzles your eyes, excited with the touching and sensing of one another swimming by.

Happy in your thoughts, you reach the entrance of the cave. The whole area is littered with a complex eco system. You look in amazement as an experienced diver would; you have never witnessed such beauty. The coral reef is breath-taking, with the colours of deep reds, vibrant oranges, lightly floating indigos, greens of freshly cut grass and yellow star fish that wave with one tentacle. You feel the warm-hearted feeling of acceptance as you enter the mouth of the cave.

You turn your deep sea torch on, the one that is on your head, reserving the batteries in the hand-held as you venture slowly into the revealing of an underwater network of tunnels. A whirling pocket of disturbing air rushes past your senses in order to escape from the deep.

Dancing cephalopods accompany your decent, while performing a luminescent hypnotic show. Captivated, you dim your head torch and follow the serenity of the glowing movements of the deep. Your eyelids are heavy and your heart is warm. Deeper you go and soon your sense of direction is lost to the creatures that guided you. Focusing on your air tank gauge, a sigh of relief and trust fills your heart, finger tips, feet and jaw.

The vast floor, walls and ceiling of the huge tunnel seem to be abundantly blessed with an array of life: jellyfish glowing red and pale blues with tentacles flashing orange, green, blue and yellow and snakes with glowing beacons under their jaw. Movements of luminescent anemones switching on and off like a synchronised warp through a wormhole, slowly guiding your movements through the centre of the tunnels.

Little oxidizing bubbles, that were trapped, float to the ceiling of the tunnel as you negotiate some of the tighter corners with the movement of your mass. Feeling the vibrations on your arm alerts you that your air is running out. You need to reserve your oxygen as you still have a network of beautiful tunnels to negotiate.

Breathe in deeply to thirty percent lung capacity, slowly and exhale calmly. Focus your mind's eye on focusing with body awareness. Turning to where you advanced previously a cold heavy drop in your throat, heart and stomach hits you like being winded. A vast wall is all around, sealing you in a cave of over two hundred meters squared. You panic and your mind drifts to a time where you felt the feeling of abandonment. Your legs and hands become numb and your focus dims. Floating there in the dark, the feelings of abandonment drawing in, you sigh with the weakness in your shoulders and the limpness in your legs become more. Slowly raising your head, you remember to reserve your oxygen by centring yourself.

Switching your hand torch on, you stare out of your eyes, to where rows upon rows of giant mineral pillows stand hidden away from the world. A shiver shoots up your spine as you feel goose pimples all over your skin, a 'treasure' that only you bear witness to.

Calm in your breathing, you look directly underneath you, finding a giant sea turtle uninterruptedly eating the plant life from the wall.

"If he got in here, I can get out" you think to yourself, but sea turtle can hold their breath for several hours depending on their activity. You guess the turtle had been there for a while as the buffet of living organisms on the shelf had almost been finished. No time to wait around for a fellow adventurer to guide the way as there is only a short time before being poisoned by the lack of oxygen.

You drop several meters to explore the ancient rocks (bones) of the Earth, hoping to see where the water pressure entered, filling this mammoth of a cave. Exhale your oxygen to ten percent lung capacity slowly, without holding your breath. This will help you sink as your lungs filled with oxygen will keep you buoyant.

You feel your body sinking with every slow exhalation of oxygen. Remember not to breathe in deeply as you will float and increase your buoyancy!

At a depth you notice a strange life form in the deep. This creature of the deep has your imagination alert! You hover in amazement as you can't work out what the creature looks like! You have no record of such shapes or beautiful colours of design. Never has this creature been recorded or seen by human eyes, you think to yourself as you pull your camera from your side and marvel at this discovery you have made, trying to give it a name.

Slowly, exhaling once again, you drop down forever into the deep below. Accompanied by yellow flickering lights that bleep from the creatures of the deep, you feel slight swirling movements from the still water that courses through the network of unseen tunnels. These swirls are coupled with the sounds of rushing water that pass your ears. These sounds increase intensely and soon are hard to bear as a feeling of many things moving at once in a tunnel beneath you like a stampede echoes through every cell in your body.

Fear rapidly fills the cave and your hands and feet start to tingle with pins and needles. The darkness of the water becomes more aggressive and your psyche is tossed to and fro, you become dazed from the blow. As you come around, the atmosphere seems calm and still but a sense of worry rushes up behind you, a feeling that you are being pursued in the deepest, darkest bowels of space. Your face goes pale with the notion of uncertainty, glowing flashes whizz by with the haste of meaning. Fish with blood red eyes squeeze their bodies into the tightest of cracks. You sense fear gripping tight in your back, your skin and hairs stand on end then shouts "Run!" A burst of energy compels you to make a dash for cover behind a mineral pillow. Your heart is thumping and the cold of the deep is starting to take a grip as you tremble.

The oxygen that once gave life has started to deplete. A massive shadow is felt overhead and a flurry of fish whizz past enhancing your sense of fear. You sit waiting with your heart in your mouth, clenching your fists tightly shut, trying to be as quiet as possible in the darkest corner of the cave. Hearing a sound you turn and a spike presses into your back. You yell out, with oxygen bubbles floating overhead. You feel the shadow pressing closer and closer, you can hardly bear the pain and the horror that awaits, but it is only the passing of your friendly turtle.

Breathe very shallow and calmly, with five percent lung capacity. There is no time to think as your oxygen is running dangerously low. Your giant friend is well out of sight by this time, but the pulling feeling on your skin of the turtle's wake is still present.

Feeling the pull and sensing the disturbance of the life forms around the walls of the tunnels, you scramble through the halls and passageways of life, and emerge from the mouth that once intrigued you. Frantically, with total exhaustion, you cup the water in desperation to move faster; feeling as if your chest is going to explode. The shimmering patterns of golden light of the tide progressively become brighter in the blue ocean, but that is not what you are looking for as the pressure builds in your face from the lack of oxygen.

Finally, finding the rope that attaches to your boat, you scramble to the midway point which is labelled green so as to pressurise yourself. The breath should be a spark in the nose at this point, at zero percent! You focus in-between the eyebrows. Your lungs are screaming for the God-given life of breath. You pull your body frantically up the rope, tearing the skin from your hands in total desperation, you break the surface of the water and breathe and cry and shout with full emotions.

Staring at the cloudless blue sky above, the smell of the fresh air and the heat of the Sun on your skin, you thank Titan, the God of the sea, for your life and the world that you just witnessed. *Breathing is key.*

Channelling Energy using Mirrors into Your Being

Knowing the true characters of your Chakras will be your guidance. Countless experiments and mathematical explanations from the greatest minds that have ever existed have said factually that energy cannot be destroyed, only transferred.

'Memorize, memorize, mesmerize. Memorize, memorize, mesmerize!'

Energy can not only be transferred, but commanded. All ancient books and scripture say you need a question to be able to find an answer. Great leaders all work on the basis of following in greatness, and then we have great leaders that share their images which resonate with the hopes and dreams of the less creative mindsets.

There are many practices of beliefs of channelling souls, Gods, demons but all these so called apparitional, conjurings are indeed a much understood practice of tapping into the frequencies of the existing or departed. As we understand it, energy transfers through the dedication of the devotee wielding the desire. Training under the workings of former master of higher education or not, fuses a geometrical configuration pattern within the brain, bringing forth a successor to the former works for great historical figures' previous art of consciousness.

When and as we explore the world of the many subjects we find the teachings of the experienced advising us to find a role-model, to embody their methods as a guide-line in creating the foundation of your future selves. We might not continue using their particular inspirational effects that once touched our needs at that time but we did indeed learn how to be ourselves through the teachings of these model types or archetypes.

Channelling is connecting to a frequency of consciousness and translating this energy into various forms of expression. The word 'channelling' says it all; channelling is opening a 'channel' to a frequency, much as you do when you tune into a television or a radio station. The channelling can be expressed in thoughts, images, spoken or written words, sounds, sensation or knowing.

Most importantly, in the knowledge of channelling a frequency, this frequency needs to be in line with your true alignment of characters. If you try and fuse a motivational figure to your inability to relate then your efforts will be futile.

Channelling is not a race in which you can become that exact frequency instantaneously. We need to crawl before we can walk, and we need to walk before we can run. We do indeed get moments of genius where guidance is sent to help us see our path. You cannot expect to sit at home and wait for the world to come to you. You must go and apply what is in your heart, whether it be meditation applied or otherwise.

Being fused to a society that rises from the hours of slumber then puts on the mindset of work, parenting etc., orientates frictions within the mind.

This is our mindset of the day, time, hours, but as our bodies need to recharge, we fall into the creational world of sleep, which is indeed the nightly socially programmed hours of slumber.

The night offers a great time for meditation, to cast your wishes or gaze up into the night sky, as the frequencies of the dense human population have relaxed their worries within the world. The world of frequency turns to a creative spark on the continent on which you reside as the confusion, hustle and bustle of life becomes calm, and the channels of hope and dreams are opened. This helps to channel good energy.

Observing, which in turn brings understanding to the world around us, offers some insight of the best times to use our chants or prayers.

Stand or sit in front of a mirror, naked or not, with dimmed lights or candles. Focus on your motivational figure.

Concentrate all your focus on the interest, task or desire. Find the place where you feel the presence of answers and relief. Use an inspirational figure that motivates you, with purest of intention within the sacred Sacrum Chakra.

As you focus on your being reflecting back at you, inhale, focusing internally in-between the eyebrows so as not to go cross-eyed. Recognise your skeletal structure, *take your time:* the flesh that covers your skeleton, the colour of your skin, eyes and hair, the dimensions of your structure, your uniqueness. As you do these inhalations, notice the calm that fills your world. Clear your mind and then ask the question or questions. Imagine you are filling your being with the answers and, frequencies you desire. See your skin glowing with this knowing.

When focusing on your dimensions, bringing your focus to your innocent eyes, you will notice that your face will change as your individual eyes will constantly adjust to the light processed by them. Don't fall prey to the lesser faces you see flashing on and off, rather focus on your innocent eyes and deeper levels of virtue for deep guidance. This meditation of innocence of intention should be carried out at sunrise, sunset or, alternatively, under candle light. Always ask the flame to guide you towards the purity of expression at which you wish to emit. The event horizon is a gateway to see life for what life is, be nurtured by it and nurture it!

The mirror does one of several things: one being that ultra violet light emitted through frequency out of the body bounces back, filtering through and empowering your body. You become the reflection that you are emitting. When we stare into a mirror we're faced with our insecurities. If we can mediate with the purest of innocent intention and accept oneself while doing this, the motivations intended can of course become one with us, because we tend to evolve when our environment changes.

Generally, when we talk about the environments, our minds instinctively process the land beneath our feet and the sky above our heads. However, what we fail to realise is that there are chemical, cellular, emotional, energetic etc. environments within every human, animal, plant, creature, planet and galaxy within this universe.

Imbalanced environments within the body can bring about stress, depression, disease, split personalities, hallucinogenic imagery etc. and can even lead to mutation.

Progressing throughout the ages as a species we have become, *once again,* very transcendentally bodily aware.

When we look into our innocent eyes in a mirror, we immediately relate one with the desires as our reflection is apparent when chanting. We have all heard stories of incantations that are told on specific days (Summer Solstice as a generic common example) with a specific number of times we chant into a mirror. As we chant into a mirror we accelerate the process of accepting frequencies with practice.

Activity:

Relax the eyes and separate them from your mind. Let your eyes process the reflection of you and the photons that enter your eyes and into your centred focus. Try not to blink. Bring your mind into your vision board, experience the energies of the world that you desire. Remember to use all your senses. Feel the sense of your energy, hopes and will going out into the distance within the universe, centring your focus. Feel the expansion of the universe pulling your energy outward, into your world that is forever expanding into experiences far greater than you have ever experienced before.

Hear your name being called out by a loved one within your perfect world. Make the association of your name with the kindest and most loving words when talked about. Hear your name and feel the presence of your name within your vision. Breathe in deeply and say, "I am alive".

The Power in a Name

What's in a name? That which we call a rose by any other name would smell as sweet. - William Shakespeare

There has never yet been a man in our history who led a life of ease whose name is worth remembering. - Theodore Roosevelt

If there is not a war, you don't get the great general; if there is not a great occasion, you don't get the great statement; If Lincoln lived in a time of peace, no one would have known his name. - Theodore Roosevelt

Bob Marley isn't my name. I don't even know my name yet. - Bob Marley

Names contain power. Ancient myths of East and West tell of a power held in one's name.

To know someone's (usually a God, Goddess or some spirits) name was to hold power over it. Think about your own name for a second. It's so powerful that your brain can process someone saying your name across a noisy crowded room.

Names contain a mass of energetic emotional charge. All these emotions - some uplifting, some disheartening - are stored into a single focal point - your name. Say your full name out loud and you can feel the emotions contained within this powerful symbol. Do you feel proud and confident in your name, or insecure and even ashamed? For example, if you were bad, your parents would shout out your name and you would be fearful.

In some ancient cultures, you were given a child-name at birth, and then later received your adult name when you reached an age of maturity. This practice helps let go of the association to the ruled adolescent years (Bodsworth 2003).

I think this was a very effective custom designed to help each person discard the childish identity attached to his/her name, along with the sense of insecurity and powerlessness attached to it, and become a strong adult who is part of the community.

As we learn to let go of the names surrounding our lives, we focus on their emotional connection, by realising the effects of the many words around us and their energetic emotional associations.

Try to remember to use your name in conjunction with uplifting phrases. Treat your name as sacred, because it is. When addressing or introducing, treat other people's names in the same way. Never use them without attaching to them some positive emotions.

The Phoenix

In ancient Greece, the Phoenix became established as a symbol of the nation's rebirth during the Greek War of Independence. It was first used in the flags of Alexander Ypsilantis, and was chosen as the official emblem of the Provisional Government (1828–1832) by Governor John Capodistria, who also named the first Modern Greek currency "Phoenix". Despite being replaced by a Germanic royal Coat of Arms, it remained a popular symbol, and was used again in the 1930s by the Second Hellenic Republic. However, its use by the military junta of 1967-1974 made it extremely unpopular, and it has almost disappeared from use after 1974, with the notable exception of the Order of the Phoenix, the country's second-highest award.

In ancient Arabic tradition, the Ghoghnus is a bird having some mythical relationship with the date palm. The Ghoghnus is said to have laid only one egg. It lived in the Arabian Desert many thousands of years ago. The word Anka comes from the word for "necklace", for the bird's neck is covered with white feathers forming like a necklace (Van der Broek, 1972).

The heightened state of awareness activating elemental states has the Phoenix as a symbolic character of new birth to countless motivations recorded throughout history!

The Phoenix is a mythical bird that is a metaphor for a specific energy that is emitted from individual groups of spiritual beliefs or specific ways of governing specific emotional outcomes (rituals). We know this because we see the patterns of how different travellers from distant lands using the symbolic energies of what that spiritual, religious (energetic emotional formula) worship is as a rebirth, the Phoenix (Van der Broek, 1972).

Some religions have beliefs in angels; these are human in form with wings to denote their spiritual position. There are dragons that fly and breathe fire in Japan. There are also other beliefs that fairies and ogres, trolls and witch craft, voodoo etc. exist. All are spiritual worship of governing a frequency of the elemental information that is held as a constant, by imagery and the power of language, with sound and the natural materials of Mother Earth!

As we learn to discover the observer's world around us, we soon realise that understanding is seeing. For us to be separate from religion or any spiritual worship we cut that part of ourselves from understanding the different types and ways we can achieve a real connection with our identity of oneself. As we lose connection we bring trauma to the body.

While writing this book I gazed from my window, finding regular visitors. I observed a magpie in its proud colours of white and black, a black and white cat along with a white and black dog. These were my frequent visitors throughout my many days of writing.

Metamorphosis is a change from one form to another, some argue a constant evolution of format in perception. We can see this in the modern age, with the progression of technology and the battle strategies of history, the many mood swings that captivate and seize the moment of rich harmonies etc.

By learning to believe that magic is in the world around us, we use our observations in order to see the mutations in everyday life.

We all live our lives based on beliefs. We model our beliefs on the many subjects. These would be work, social, dreams, spiritual or passive beliefs, but all are leading you in a belief that you'll get there, wherever 'there' is.

Metamorphosis or mutation comes in the form of a Phoenix in this spiritual ritual, when there is a dip in morality, belief or a dream that one wants to experience. This can be explained by the motivations of great leaders and the symbolic drive they offer the following parties, civilisations etc. The trust in hope becomes the elemental frequency of the following parties (the masses) thus creating the optimum amount of energy to create the leader's vision and acceptance of the desired outcome of the masses!

Example of realisation: Do you think the highest possible government 'weapon' is a nuclear missile or a laser, that can fuse and repair a panel on the side of a space craft outside the outer reaches of our planet's ozone layer, where there is a vacuum?

The real prize is the creational transcendental workings of the embodied elemental beings that discovered or meditated the creational information of invention. You are the creational minds that created $E=mc^2$, which gave birth to nuclear energy, and then got manipulated in the creation of the Atom bomb etc.

The ozone layer was discovered in 1913 by the French physicists Charles Fairy and Henri Buisson. The ozone layer is a layer in Earth's atmosphere which contains relatively high concentrations of ozone (O_3). This layer absorbs 97–99% of the Sun's high frequency ultraviolet light.

The first electric washing machine appeared in 1901 thanks to Alva Fisher. By applying a motor, she made a container of water and soap move the way a washer does today.

I am talking to you, the person reading these words, "You are the creation, you are the technology."

Ink is a liquid or paste that contains pigments and/or dyes and is used to colour a surface to produce an image, text, or design. Ink is used for drawing and/or writing with a pen, brush, or quill. Thicker inks, in paste form, are used extensively in letterpress and Lithographic printing.

Many ancient cultures around the world have independently discovered and formulated inks for the purposes of writing and drawing. We don't all arrive at the discovery at the same time. Most of us are lost in battle of continuous cycles for generations, but knowing that the many routes that have guided the Elders on their stages of conscious awareness are laid bare, you can observe and free yourself as the creational beings that *YOU* are.

Guided Meditation

The Phoenix is symbolically fused to the concept of re-birth. The symbolic power of the visual, verbal and rhythmical emotion has already been set by the past conscious beings of our history. We observe that the car you drive or the pavements you walk upon are that of the old conscious mind-sets.

Whether being dreams of light works in heart or other, gives us solid evidence of a visual idea that it historically exists, because you can go outside and touch the concrete floor with your hand and you can drive the complex 'mathematical number' that becomes energy in motion - the car!

If the floor that you walk on gives you the feeling of support and the car that you drive gives you the feeling of independence etc., why can't a symbolic idea of a Phoenix give re-birth to individuals, communities and nations? The answer is, *it does*. Remember, your focusing in the mind's eye is a different dimension. If we think it and believe it or even empower people by the concept of it, it will indeed wake up.

Meditation

Activity:

This meditation must be performed in the direct contact of the sunrise and sunset. Find, by looking at your surroundings, that you have gravitated to your meditation site! This place is where you can relax and feel the true you.

Sit with your feet flat on the floor or crossed legged. Keep your back straight as the flow of natural melodies of information can emit from your being. Separate your eyes, mind and third eye by looking at the inside of your eye lids and focusing in the centre of light.

When your eyes of mind become separated, draw your mind to your desired vision of the creative perception. By this point you should have memorised the interlocking, musical game play of your vision board, emotionally, physically and mentally. Now, with that centred soulful focus, each sentence below holds rhymes of coloured information. Relate all melodies of information to where you feel it emitting within and without your vision board!

Relaxed, sitting in this feeling of warmth, your heart becomes aware of your sense of being. By inhaling this healing energy fully, directing it into the Third Eye, you exhale fully, settling into calm assertive serenity at the Base Chakra with the word 'peace'.

When ready, slowly feel the energy channelling up from the centre of Mother Earth into your Second Sacrum Chakra. Feel the deep trust you have with the unquestioned belief that your energy 'YOU' is leading 'YOU' to where 'YOU' desire to be at your Sacred Sacrum Chakra.

Push your settled trust melody of information down into your Base Chakra, where you connect *continually* to your expanding senses of service. Slowly bring this attentive attention down to your feet or seated position, and into whatever is touching the ground as an anchor in this realm!

Feel the support and trust in the Earth beneath you, birthing your awareness back up from the centre of the earth, into the Base and Sacred Sacrum Chakra with the feeling of your sense of trust in fertility. Continually, to keep your focus of musical awareness, rising up into the Solar Plexus, a sense of light acceptance enters your being at this point, the acceptance of everything around you, bit by bit, is changing into the perception of what you desire.

With the deep simplistic feeling desiring this service, you bring your focus back into your sacred Sacrum Chakra of trust. Now you can trust in knowing that your energy is leading you to exactly where you desire to be, filtering into the Base Chakra of anchoring senses, and down through the legs and onto the ground beneath you.

Feel the support, trust and acceptance in the earth beneath you. Bring your awareness back up into the Base, Sacred Sacrum and Solar-Plexus Chakras, with the feeling of your senses, trust in the universe and acceptance of pure light.

From the ground beneath, you feel a channel of two hearts becoming one. The trust and acceptance of laughter moves higher into the Heart Chakra, where the feeling of beauty and love is felt abundantly in the heart. This light and heavy feeling of love and beauty flows into your healing hands. Feel your heart pumping a song of clarity, tranquillity, compassion, mercy out into and past the end of creation, as your awareness focuses on the blood that is pumping around your body with every heartbeat, pushing love and beauty around your being.

Remember to focus on where love and beauty exists within your vision board, and give equal energetic emotion of service to it. To serve yourself is to acknowledge a desired realm is a better place for you to serve!

Continually hearing the love and beauty pumping around your body, you push once again down into the acceptance, trust, earthly anchored senses and through the deep rooted connection onto the ground beneath you.

Feel the support, trust, acceptance and beautiful love in the earth beneath you, dissolving any slight harmonics that don't touch your creative expansion at this time! Bring your awareness back up into the Base, sacred Sacrum, Solar-Plexus and Heart Chakras with the feeling of your senses, trust, acceptance and beautiful love.

Inhale fully with the intention that healing is already a part of you, and exhale fully. Do this for twenty cycles while bringing your awareness to the blood that pumps around your body. Every time you breathe inward, momentarily open your eyes to the early morning, low light of the life giving sun.

From the ground beneath, you feel a channel of sensation of atmosphere all around, a mythical, enchanting rhythm of music entwined with all that you are. Trusting in the truth of fertility you accept this audience of knowing as the beautiful love moves higher into the Throat Chakra, where the feeling of excitement is felt. This feeling transports you to a time where your voice is being heard in your vision board.

This time, where your voice is being heard as your ultimate expression, you feel the beautiful love in your heart, the acceptance within your Solar Plexus, the trust that your energy is leading you to your destination of desire with the sense of feeling it now, down through the legs into the ground beneath you.

Feel the support, trust, acceptance, beautiful love and excitement of your voice on the earth beneath you, bringing your awareness back up from the ground beneath and within you. Feel a channel of energetic energy flow into the Base, Sacrum, Solar-Plexus, Heart and Throat Chakras with the feeling of your senses, trust, acceptance beautiful love and excitement.

Inhale fully as you open your eyes momentarily, focusing in-between the eyebrows, and exhale fully, closing your eyes to the moving of the low light of the morning's life-giving sun. Do this for thirty cycles while bringing your awareness to the blood that pumps around your body. Feeling this life of the sun shining out of you by this point, you radiate, like the sun, healing other people who see the sun's rays emitting out of you, for them to heal alongside as we share this journey together.

This channel of energetic energy in motion continues up into the Third Eye Chakra, where all the images you hold as a constant are playing out in the dimensional mind. You feel the happiness of service to this place as you walk through your internal world, *continuing* to focus in-between the eyebrows. With the excitement and beautiful love that each moment brings, feel the acceptance and trust in every action that plays out. Hear your name being called as you touch a physical object within your internal realm.

Feel your emotional energy continually playing out within your being as you connect through your legs to the floor beneath you. Feel the support, trust, acceptance, beautiful love, excitement and happiness of the images you hold within your internal world on the earth beneath you. Bring your awareness back up into the Base, Sacred Sacrum, Solar-Plexus, Heart, Throat and Third Eye Chakras with the feeling of your senses, trust, acceptance, beautiful love, excitement and happiness.

Inhale fully, opening your eyes momentarily to the early low light of the morning's life-giving sun, and exhale fully for ten long cleansing cycles while bringing your awareness to the blood that pumps around your body. The focus on the blood should have changed state by this point to a movement of the dual, co-existence of the energy body, this pumping glow of 'light works', manifests very quickly with pure intentions of exercise!

Continuing with the connection you have by channelling your focus of awareness at the top of your head (Crown Chakra) this energetic opening of information is that of Relief, relief with the sense of detecting distance. Relief with the sense of detecting distance, of the ever unfolding, un-grasping expansion of the universe around and within you, and the knowing that a higher being works through you, leads to us becoming more and more energetically connected to all the ecosystems.

Do not try to think, just feel, sense energetically what is in the moment of heavenly ascensions. Your subconscious mind will find the correct connectional conscious patterns toward complete awareness.

With the sense of expansion coupled with relief, bring your focus down into the happiness of melody in the ever waking moment within the mind's eye. Feel the excitement of what you have learnt, accept your breath, enforcing this by the trust in your senses that they are guiding you towards your future desires. Push this energy down through your rooted legs, onto the ground beneath you.

Feel the support, trust, acceptance, beautiful love, excitement, happiness and relief, coupled with sensing distance of the ever expanding universe on the earth beneath you. Bring your awareness back up into the Base, Sacred Sacrum, Solar-Plexus, Heart, Throat, Third Eye and Crown Chakras with the feeling of your senses, trust, acceptance, beautiful love, excitement, happiness and relief as you picture yourself sitting on stars.

As we become more aware of the energetic musical information of each Chakra, equalling relief, we open the bodily temple as a starting point. This opening of gates connects the ever expanding self (universe) to the earthly senses (ultimate expression). This is called centring, balancing, Earthly or Heavenly ascension.

The symbolic nature of a Phoenix is to re-enter new emotional information into the Chakra points (vortexes) of energy called a rebirth, by using this symbol with the symbolic power that resonates with your individual characters. In this case we are using the Phoenix to burn an image onto the retina and mind's eye.

The dual co-existence of information is: your earthly bodily senses, peace, trust, acceptance, beautiful love, excitement, happiness and relief, as a starting place!

As we focus on our desires, we tend to find it slow at first but then without realising it, everything comes at once! You say to yourself, "Something has to go wrong", because we are in the habit of expecting bad things around the corner. The truth is that, as we are on the road to success, there are many side roads that have *levels* of attraction. We travel along our true path but then see a desirable pit-stop, being an attractive male or female, other interests of business etc. These pit-stops can be enjoyed, but are just that 'pit-stops'. People can stay in them for years, or even a life time, thinking of their true path.

A dream lived or a desire experienced touches every ounce of our being with the motivation to live in that moment, but that moment is only a part of the bigger picture. We learn in the moment and let it help us push forward toward the path intended, and not be held up in the pit-stops of rebirth, but the end destination of your true rebirth, 'identity' awaits with the entire vision as a reality.

A mighty ancient flowing river that was forged by the hand of the Supreme Being can indeed be stopped by a dam and redirected with the engineering of creational individuals! With the river newly redirected, it finds itself at the exact destination, the sea or oceans. Do not think you are too old or too settled to continue with what you forged, but then got held up at a dam or pit stop; energy just wants to flow *so let it be*. You believe in YOU remember.

Sins of the Mind

One Saturday night, after a leisurely stroll, I walked past a little treasure in the middle of the city. This place of places often has my heart with its lake that breathes life to the many swans, Canada Geese, ducks and other descended dinosaurs. I have witnessed these amazing beings from freshly hatching to entering adolescence, taking their first flight under wing and chattering with their neighbours. The giant Oak trees and the curtains of the Willow trees are deep in green foliage, while the Fir trees give shelter to the abundant wildlife living here. Gazing up at the stars for an hour or so, feeling at peace with the sounds of the night, I planned to spend the following day here. My day of rest would have much time to contemplate my weekly observations.

Eagerly, I woke early the next morning with the sun shining through my open windows, the wind moving my curtains softly while every colour of the fresh morning light enhanced my mood as I stepped out the door. I found myself wide-eyed with a smile from ear to ear, peacefully walking along the orange stone path surrounded by the freshly cut green grass. Right on schedule the joggers passed with their timely minute breaks as they paced on the spot. Inquisitive dogs sniffed out the territorial areas that other canines marked earlier. With myself now happily perched at the top of the nearby hill next to my meditation partner; a giant Oak tree, unfolding a patterned blanket, I lay it to rest on the floor along with a good book and lunch for the day. From this vantage spot the whole park breathes with life.

Sitting in solitude with my legs crossed, I saw returning Canadian Geese swooping down from the horizon, following the ley-lines of the land. Touching down, breaking the water's surface of the lake, the spray from their webbed feet cooled the air as they chatter amongst themselves, settling within the wildlife. Feeling the proud sense of every living being coexisting in the moment, I slowly closed my eyes to feel the sun's rays upon my face and the gentle breeze stroking my skin with the warm touch of summer. Inhaling fully, feeling the fresh morning air opening my lungs, I focused in-between my eyebrows. Then, exhaling, I brought my awareness to my senses of this area into my trust of laughter, acceptance in letting go, love and beauty in the moment, excitement in settling, sensing rhythmical harmonics in bridging them all together in a conscious tunnelling, with the intention to travel into my mind's eye then finally breathing relief sinking deeper into my subconscious mind. By this time my breathing was very shallow to where my breath and focus flashed together in-between my eyebrows.

Suddenly, feeling my head drop quickly brought my eyes to attention. It was completely dark. I must have fallen asleep and missed the whole day thinking aloud. Looking around alertly, there wasn't a single person in sight. Confused, I stood up, with my legs sore from sitting for a prolonged time. Stretching out, while inhaling and staring deep into the night sky, the air tasted slightly bitter, a complete change from the basking that I remembered from earlier. Gathering some of my belongings from a well-planned stay in the park,

I saw a shadow on the far side of the lake where the exit to my vehicle awaited my cautious driving. Relieved to know that I wasn't alone in the park, my eyes panned back to the objects next to me. To my surprise, all the food that I brought was covered in ants and flies, not fit for man nor beast. I left them and walked towards my chariot.

Walking down the steep decline the wind timely edged a high pitch. The night seemed to be not what I had experienced in this place, my sanctuary. The bushes either side had the most impulsive nature that filled me with a twinge of fear. The stirring wind gusted erratically, trying to take my belongings from my gripping hands. I continued with haste to grapple against the wind towards my car, passing to where I had seen the shadow from earlier. I quickly located the key then sat in the car peering out of the windows whilst hurrying to start the engine. With no hesitation I quickly drove away.

On the journey home, feeling a sense of urgency whilst pulling up at a set of traffic lights, a huge truck slowly pulls up, towering along-side. The truck itself and driver has no regard for your small, insignificant self. As he takes a long pull on his cigar, the smoke bellows out blowing in the wind and through a slight opening in the window hits my lungs with the foul taste of smoke and fuel as he pulls away from the traffic lights. Winding the window up, choking as the vehicle becomes engulfed in a thick cloud of black toxic smog, my mind settles into a low mood as the drive home is a long and methodical one. Turning the key brings silence to the front of the apartment as I step out onto the driveway, one foot, then two feet walk and enter my home. Up the stairs with a heavy head, hitting the bed, a bitter taste in the back of my throat reminds me of the night-time scene.

This night holds no sleep of distant lands, where magical tales rejuvenate my being, only tossing and turning as the countless hours of restlessness unfolds. As the birth of the early morning pierces the land with its golden glow, a heavy heart is felt as no sounds of birds chirping or laughter from passing bodies can be heard, just the silence of people in thought. Aware of the strange unfamiliar happenings, I look around the open plan room. Slowly sitting up in bed, my eyes cast to my trusty friend, a tiny little sea turtle, which was to be donated to the Sea Life Centre when he got too big, along with dozens of tropical fish which all seemed to be hiding within the coral reef. With many questions running around the mind I ready myself for a day's work.

Commuting on the tube, as parking is impossible within the city, I hear the rustling plastic wrappers as people mantle their food and water while shovelling as much down their necks as possible, and the folding then refolding of newspapers with their bold titles and the sounds of news reporters on the speaker next to me, while their images flash on the several screens littered throughout the tube. The booming of every sound and movement is felt as my lack of sleep shows in the irritations found in the voice of the news reporter. The phrases that are used and the silence from the hundreds of passengers that have no conscious belief that another feeling human being is sitting next to them activates emotions within me.

With the exit to the heart of the city at its next stop, I rise and gather by the automatic doors. Clutching the pole that steadies my feet as people intend to be the first to exit, I feel a sense of savage primal emotions to conform to the masses funnelling me out and up the escalators to where the blissful blue sky awaits, but no time to savour the moment as people scurry and push me into the next stage of my journey, towards the four walls I call work. I find my feet standing at the front of a tall building. This building looks down from its cloudy ascension, beckoning my name then drawing me inside to where the receptionist, a middle aged woman, and her assistant, Chloe awaits.

Chloe, a young graduate with fair hair and rosy cheeks, always seems to have a kind look for everyone who enters. Passing, my eyes are drawn to her kind ways. Entering the elevator I soon arrive at the 42nd floor, a pop in my ears as the altitude changes brings my hand to the inside pocket to where I unsheathe a soft boiled sweet. Cruising through the aisles of the vast open office space, sitting down at my desk with the comfort of my trusty chair, the only sounds heard are that of thousands upon thousands of computer keys whittling away with unrelenting continuation. Breathing in, I almost hold my breath as the manager makes his rounds, beating a ruler in the palm of his hand, *slap, slap,* as the whistling sound of the flexing ruler repeatedly approaches my cubical.

"Why are you not working?" the manager fires. "Why are you not pleasant?" my startled, half shouting reply.

Grieving the very second the words touch my boss's ears, he smiles, which takes me by surprise as he never expressed emotions before. Walking off with what seems to be a hop in his step seemed puzzling.

With no haste, I boot up the computer that sits opposite, setting myself a goal to work harder that day so as to defuse my outburst. Relieved, standing in the canteen for a well-earned break, waiting patiently for my turn by the vending-machine in silence, I contemplate what might satisfy the taste buds as my stomach growls at the tuna salad baguette. There is much time to contemplate matters while looking around the room at the grey, black and white uniforms. The movements of papers seem to be hypnotising while gazing at the hundreds of synchronised co-workers grazing and drinking their harvests. Half focused on the vending-machine and the silence, I step forwards towards the tuna salad baguette but clumsily bump into an attractive co-worker carrying a hot cup of tea. The hot tea slightly spills and burns only myself. In a flash, I uncontrollably apologise and offer to buy a second cup of tea but this falls on deaf ears. With a remark, "Oh, you idiot!" the co-worker walks off and idly talks amongst the group as they set their eyes upon me. The feeling of unease unsettles my mood of nothingness, so I retreat to my cubical, passing the manager who nods with a slight smile.

Barely turning the corner, I hear my boss's voice shouting out my name. Approaching with heavy breathing, he announces; "I forget to mention, you are being transferred." "What?" catching my breath. "Yes, I know it's a little sudden and I know this is the first you have heard about this, as I put your name forward this morning, the powers that be want you to go overseas to an outlet we have there."

"But, but..." are the only words that fall out of my mouth. "Yes, yes... all your expenses are paid for, tickets booked and you leave within two days. Be sure to arrange everything before you go!" enforcing his authority.

"How long is this overseas business trip?" I ask. "Three weeks starting the 31st."

Contemplating the break from this lifeless place gives me strong hope. As I solidly agree to the offer, in-turn he hands me an envelope titled my name, relaying a message as his voice fades down the aisle.

"There will be several things you need to take care of on your first day, so be sure to expect a work load" he remarks, returning to his endeavours.

Illuminated, I gather my belongings and pass the assistant receptionist with a spring in my step and a smile on my face, to which she responds with a smile. Feeling expressive, I set off home with two days to prepare. Exiting the building, I notice the idle talkers from the canteen huddled together in a white cloud of smoke. Their eyes locate me with the exhaling smoke from their nostrils seeming to dam my very existence. So I wave and, hesitantly, they half raise their hands then sink back into the cloud of smoke.

Bidding farewell to my pet turtle and many fish, I hand the keys to my apartment to my very excited sister. I agree to rent the apartment, while away for the duration of my unexpected overseas exploration, under one condition: to have consideration for the elderly people in the complex, as I had gained good rapport with them.

With the parting pleasantries over, I find myself boarding then ushered to the location of the seating area onboard the plane. This brought a sense of adventure, as the last overseas business venture that I had, had been a logistical meeting that lasted one night several months prior to this. The thought of what awaited within these three weeks had all the nerves in my belly fluttering with anticipation, a real break away from the well fused cycles that had been my life for so long now.

The flight was long and restful with slight turbulence at times, which didn't seem to bother the other passengers as they ate and drank freely and openly with the waving hands beckoning for another serving. At this point, my mind drifted back to the canteen days before, with the red tea mark still sensitive on my chest. Suddenly, shaking my head thinking "Why am I thinking of that incident?" I shift my attention to the window and the many layers of cotton wool clouds, so serenely thinking as I become docile, like in a trance. A loud ping from the speakers next to me sparks my awareness, as the announcement broadcasts that we have just entered Chinese air space and will be landing shortly.

As efficient as the logistics of airborne people carriers are, we safely land to where I come into the company of a well dressed, well spoken translator and company driver. Their cultural greetings consisted of bowing of the head, which I had read partly during the long overseas flight, and still half docile I make a hand gesture towards the exit. In reply they bow their heads and my baggage is taken to the vehicle.

Hong Kong is one of the most densely populated areas in the world, with a land mass of 1,104 km^2 (426 sq. miles) and a population of seven million people, 95% ethnic Chinese and 5% from other groups. This was apparent as we drove towards the 5 star hotel in central Hong Kong, "the city that never sleeps", the translator says as we make conversation.

This place, outside of the window, had a barren hustle bustle look to it, a mighty change to my humble apartment that was left behind. Wondering "What have I gotten myself into?" a hand from the translator touches my shoulder asking how I felt. There must have been a look of confusion on my face. "I feel nothing" I said. "Oh you feeling nothing!" replied the translator.

The following day, waking from a blissful sleep amongst the finest of silk bed linen, with the air conditioner and freshly cut flowers filling the room with a fresh heavenly taste, a newly pressed suit awaited, hung over the Chinese-style folding dressing screen. What a blissful sight, but a question remains in my mind from the passing evening: "How do you feel?" But still feeling nothing, I look around the room to where a Chinese Orchid had been nicely presented on the table. The cultural differences are all just a visual, which were half expected from advertisements and documentaries I had seen over the years.

It was 5:30am local time. Remembering that there were several things to take care of today, and not knowing what might be required first, I leap out of bed and quickly shower. Half way through showering the telephone rings out. Then the door knocks. "Room service!" The smell from the food breaches the gap in the bathroom door and over the shower screen, triggering my mouth to water, hopping around trying to cover my foot with a sock. The food is good but there isn't time to finish it as the Chinese like an early start.

Not wanting to bring a bad name to the company's reputation, I find myself waiting in the lobby straightening out the collars of my freshly pressed suit. I look over to the reception area with its cylindrical marble pillars, leading to an open plan rest room with a grand bar. I am immediately, taken aback by the lavish reds that symbolise wealth in China, and beautifully done it was. The chairs, and tables that accompanied, house several international business-looking folk who bury their heads in newspapers. Their cultural differences were told in their posture and the many languages that titled their reading materials. Some slurping noodle soup, some devouring bagels, while others drinking earlier than expected in the day. An approaching lobby boy pauses just before the rug that the table rests on, bows his head then ushers me towards a group of international co-workers eager to meet my acquaintance. Feeling a sense of community as they talk in broken English, introductions are made and a sense of being is felt throughout the group as we make our way out of the hotel doors and towards the vehicles.

The day is much busier, with the pollution swirling from the car exhausts, while three wheeled motorcars whizz by, carrying more weight than their vehicles permit. The taste of the cigar and fumes from the previous night emerges and the towering buildings bring forth a slight insignificant feeling. We drive out of the looming city which held a phrase perched in the mind, 'Familiarity breeds contempt', meaning when a person sees the same people every day, they wind up becoming a part of your life and then they want that person to change. If someone isn't what others want them to be, the others become angry.

Everyone seems to have a clear idea of how others should lead their lives, but have no clue about his or her own. With this in mind, I keep my conversation to a minimum as we arrive at a temple where we are greeted by a Chinese man dressed in white. The party seems to have the utmost respect for this man. He leads us to a flat grass land that overlooks the blue South Chinese Sea. It was tradition to take our shoes off. With the grass soft under foot we follow, relieved to hear serenity away from the busy roads where only moments ago I stood. The translator, in a soft voice, tells me that this man in white is a highly respected Tai Chi master. Slowly we steady our pace to a halt as we began the lesson.

The movements of this man seem to flow with the wind, caught up in his rhythm I feel a tremendous weight lifting from my body as I mimic the movements, but just as this feeling of what seemed to be weightlessness was felt, the lesson is over and my feet sheathed from the ground. Bowing in respect for what this man had let me experience, left me with a curious notion: how can standing on grass, moving my arms and legs about bring, bring, I don't know how to explain it, so I ask my translator. The feeling you felt is known to the people as Chi or Qi. I am very confused. The image of going back into the city, with the thick pollution, doesn't sit well with me.

Before leaving the temple place, I separate from the group as they individually bow at a beautifully carved statue. Resting, with the city in the distance, next to blossom trees, one pink in flower and one white, a little wind strokes my interest as it carries a trail of blossom petals out to sea. As they dance with the floating tide, a man dressed in white appears next to me. Calmly he says in perfect flowing English, "Many moments pass by but only a few are observed, like the flowing petals in the wind, soon reach the surface of the waters but the memory lasts a life time".

This man clearly has been drinking too early in the day, as he didn't make much sense at all. Nodding my head, I honour his presence.

Several minutes pass in silence, then the man steps one pace forward to where I see the side of his face. This man looks around eighty yet twenty at the same time. Without moving his head a powerful message from the ages touches my ears, "I free myself not by trying to be free, but by simply noticing how I am imprisoning myself in the very moment I am imprisoning myself".

As the moment sinks into my pores, the sounds of scurrying feet approach. Shifting my attention to the translator walking down the stone path, turning back I see the man in white has vanished. Strange, but thinking no more of it, I join the well dressed and softly spoken translator as the conversation drifts to the area, I am told it is that of a burial ground of ancient monks. These monks fought bravely and were said to be the greatest warriors in Chinese history, taking on a dozen plus enemies single-handedly.

Unnoticed before, where I had stood, many flowers lay, resting on the ridge. This place did have a strange atmosphere, thinking about it. Gathering by the vehicle, ready to get my teeth stuck into work, we drive not towards the city but away from it. This seems odd, as I was under the impression that I had much to set as a foundation today. We drive, stopping only to observe the valleys and how the water flows from the great mountains. I smile courteously as the high emotions from the co-workers try to include me in every conversation, practicing their English, their hands pointing to the direction of the distant mountains.

"See, the water comes from there and flows into where we collect it in our reservoirs, *it never stops*. We have faith in the water, but this doesn't mean we let go of choice or choosing what we see in the future, it merely means we observe that the forever flowing water is our changing state of desire."

These people certainly have a way with words. Pulling up, we proceed to walk to where we find ourselves surrounded by dense bamboo at the foot of a set of stairs. The reddish stones that make up the stairs lead to a dozen single storey apartments dotted throughout the bamboo. This breath-taking scene has a single path with tall green, brightly manicured bamboo. Just before the main path, a stone bird with a golden tail stands proud where two beautifully traditionally dressed ladies greet us.

They are dressed mirroring one another perfectly in their whites and pinks. Coming off the main path are several paths that link small bridges leading to the apartment doors. Just before each bridge stands a warrior statue facing towards the main path with dozens of colourful little birds flying past, singing, following the main route.

The translator announces that we will be spending the rest of the day and evening here. To my delight, the two ladies individually take their guests into the small apartments, pausing just before the warrior statue as they chant something. I ask the translator to interpret their actions. "To ask the guardian for safe passage is to reconnect with your ancestors, to watch over you while you sleep."

As we patiently depart, while bowing and leaving our colleagues in their shelters, it soon becomes my turn to approach the warrior statue and ask for safe passage. I don't know what to say as I am not used to talking to a carved piece of stone. "The words must come from within" I am advised, looking back for reassurance. Bringing my palms together the words surprisingly come to me, "The blood that courses through these veins of mine, are that of my brothers and sister, that of my mother and father and that of my ancestors, that are you and me, I ask you brave warrior keep me safe for my time in your arms". A surge of emotional energy seems to come from deep within my belly to find tears running down my face. With a strong noble look that comes from the remaining group, I enter my spacious living quarters.

There are two rooms, the main room that houses a bed and a wash room, which has hot running water. I take a shower to contemplate my actions. Emerging from the vapour of the shower a traditional dress suit awaits me on the bed. "These people walk through walls", I think to myself, slipping on the silk garments and a pair of comfortable slippers.

Sliding the wooden panel door open, I see that it is early dusk. With torches lit and light sounds coming from down the main path, I pass the warrior statue as the flames toy with the wind. I pause slightly, whilst holding the respect that I thought I'd never have for a carved piece of stone. The main path is a very comfortable walk with benches scattered in strategic places so as to observe the beauty that this magical place has to offer. I inhale fully and exhale fully as a voice, and then a smiling face with gleaming eyes becomes my company.

"Did you enjoy your rest?" the soft voice from the translator asks. "Very refreshing", I reply, as we make our way down the main path together. I ask a personal question. "Why did I have such an emotional reaction to the statue?" half holding my breath as I thought it was a stupid question. "It is simple. When you really ask with the intent of connecting to something else rather than just yourself, you connect to the soul of the universe and the soul of the universe is you, as all is one and one is all".

I don't really understand as we join the rest of the group, with the images of myself crying in front of the statue still flashing in my mind. This brings slight embarrassment. I try to conceal my blushing cheeks as my co-workers laugh amongst themselves in front of a set of giant wooden doors. I feel the warmth and humour as they explain the character nicknames of individuals within the group. A gong sounds, bringing a happy silence, the wide doors spring open redirecting the flames from the torches and music is heard as we enter.

The space inside houses a grand fountain in the centre, where a Zheng instrument is being played. As the familiar people fan out and fill the area I notice several rooms leading off the main court yard. A Chinese woman, dressed in traditional clothing walks towards me, beckoning me to follow her.

"She is taking you for a massage" the translator informs, "this will be healing for the body and mind." Succumbing to the massage, my mind starts to wander, but just as I find myself sinking into many thoughts of emotions felt, the lady asks, "Where is your mind at?"

Explaining that my mind just so happens to be in the past, thinking of how I received the red mark on my chest, which still annoyed, to which she replies in a soft voice, "Entering the world of mind can hold many obstructions, and energy seldom flows at its most efficient, but by entering the world of mind by choice, we learn just how to hold what it is we most want as desires, we then transform everything."

These words have a lot of sense to them, as I often let my mind wander to the past or even future in times of worry. I guess that was just my auto-pilot. With the tension released in my shoulders and lower back, sitting next to the fountain, I fixate on the music playing from the most unusual instrument, the

Zheng. The musician seems to be displaying the Tai Chi movements that the Master expressed earlier in the day. It is truly beautiful to watch as the emotions are acted out in sound as well as movement.

After playing, the musician accompanies me by the soft running water from the fountain. Seeming not to notice me, he peers at his reflection in the water. Watching his actions draws me closer as he turns around to face me. Surprised, I quickly ask, "Why express such movements when playing that instrument?"

He looks at me blankly as my translator overhears and repeats my question. He smiles and sits on the fountain's edge, placing his hand into the water, disturbing the surface. "The body must have a brain to think and a body must have a fist to fight, by bringing instinct and logic together you become an unstoppable force in expressing your true self."

The next day, after waking early, I venture out, passing the benches and the extinguished torches to the centre of the bright green bamboo gardens where I had spent the remainder of the previous evening drinking Saki. The early morning greets me with the pleasant sounds of chatter, as people sit crossed legged on cushions placed on the floor. While enjoying the taste of the herbal tea in my tiny cup, a man carrying a walking stick stands. "This is my seat and it has been mine for twenty years" the voice from the small slender man comments. Humble and succumbing to the feeling of serenity from the area, I apologise and offer the seat.

Walking to a quiet spot next to the hand rail I peacefully stand. 'Tap, tap, tap' I hear coming from the floor next to me, as the man abruptly taps his walking stick. "This is my place to stand, and it has been for twenty four years." This man is clearly domineering but at that moment an image of my childhood flashes before my eyes. The image is that of a time caught being naughty as a child. Shaking it off, focusing on the old man, I then calmly bow my head while placing my tiny cup on the table, thanking the staff that served me. Stepping onto the main path, noticing the translator waving, I speedily catch up and descend the red stone stairs. While leaving the bamboo complex I gaze back at the tall stone bird with a golden tail, as I enter the vehicle once again.

We drive away from the city in conversation for about two hours, watching as the many purposely flooded fields, with their beautifully cultivated crops grow in the early morning sun. The people in the fields, arms outstretched, expanding in the direction of the sun, feed my curiosity.

"We have arrived" the translator suddenly says. This was where I was to stay for the next seven days. Confused, I look around as there isn't a single building in sight. The voice from the translator.

"You must walk in that direction alone", pointing to the mountains in the distance.

"Continue on this path but be sure to follow that peak, but before you leave I would like to tell you a story. A noble man from a noble village was sent to find the divine knowledge of power. The man travelled for many miles soon reaching the foot of a giant waterfall, frustrated with his fruitless findings he screams out with uncontrollable fury up to the heavens, collapsing to his knees, with no fight left within him he falls into the water's edge, his torso and head submerged while his legs stayed grounded. A rumble comes from the waterfall and a dragon appears, landing in the water next to him, picking up the half dead man. 'Why do you disturb my slumber?' The dragon asks the man as he looks at his reflection in the water. The limp man replies, 'I am in search of the divine knowledge of power.' The dragon laughs and places the man to his feet. Laughing the dragon sounds out, piercing the centre of the man's brain with his ancient words that carry to the truth of consciousness. The divine knowledge is knowing that the clothes you wear and the phrases of language in which you use, is a creation of the human heart, felt dual existence of mind, the divine power is bridging the creational mind duelled heart with the bodily senses, which keeps you in constant process in your external reality."

I now knew exactly what the translator was saying. The language used when I confronted my boss in the office promoted high emotions within him, but the images of being punished for expressing my true self resulted in a burnt chest in the canteen. This also happened from the embarrassment that was held from crying at the warrior statue, resulting with that rude old man in the tea house.

Waving, as the vehicle slowly fades into the distance I contemplate what exactly my job was in this barren place. Gathering my thoughts I set off in the charted direction that I had been instructed. Travelling the long road that separated the many flooded fields, I marvel at the architecture of the land and how it has been carved by human hand. The dusty path I walk was a barrier that held the water in the rice fields and the staggered fields helped the irrigation with the flowing of the water.

Feeling the exhaustion from the ever relenting gradient, I pause as a young woman in her early twenties carrying two containers of water attached to a bamboo stick approaches. She is accompanied by a little girl around seven or eight. The woman and her little sister live in a nearby village that doesn't have a well. Her family has much work to do in the rice fields and she is entrusted to take care of her sister and household duties.

The day's walk has been testing with no trees along the path to shelter from the peak of the sun. Passing the two, smiling, I make a hand gesture to drink some of their water. The young woman and girl bow their heads then sit sharing their water. I savour the taste of the refreshing water that cools me from the heat.

The young woman tells me how she imagines herself being a translator within the year, and that the land that her family have kept for some generations now has no hold in her heart. Yes she is accustomed to the valleys and trees, where she travelled and played as a child. She is accustomed to the best fishing sites that the rivers provide and she knows that if she stays in the village she will marry, have children and her future will be secure. But she knows that if she stays that she will be following the old conscious trends that have been set by her ancestors, and she wouldn't be following her heart's desires. We can all fall into the trap of putting up with the surroundings we become accustomed to, I thought, as she asks me many questions about my distant land while I honour their presence.

Relieved for the water and conversation, I thank the girls. As smiles are exchanged for their generosity and refreshing mood, the girl asks, "Why are you walking these plains?"

"I am in search of a building to start my work" I explain, "I must follow the peak of that mountain," pointing to the distance.

She doesn't reply, while standing to her feet and continuing in the direction that I saw them travelling. "Did I say something wrong?' I ask the young woman, as they reach ten feet away from me. She turns and says, "This is my empire, yes I follow a common wealth, as this is our land but I stand on my feet that touch the earth, I feel the support that grounds me to the earth, and I have the mind to find water and food when my people need it so."

With that she waves and I press forward towards the base of the mountain's peak. The day slowly weaves on to where three monks are surrounding a little camp fire. The glistening embers coupled with the sounds of the night float off in the early fall of dusk as I accompany them.

"Good evening, we have been expecting your arrival" one of the monks comments in an American accent. Surprised, I ask "You're American?"

"Yes one of our temples is based in that beautiful country, I studied there as a child while continuing with my ancestral teachings" he replied.

We continue talking amongst the group, finding that one monk had been raised in England and the other in India.

Extinguishing the fire, we set off toward the mountains in the distance. The monks have a warm glow that I can't quite understand but it seems to energise my tired legs. As we round a corner, I look down at the open scene of endless fields of skyscraper-high pillars, which clearly had been the dried surface of the bottom of the ocean some millions of year ago.

The monk looks across the land, telling me how a great battle had taken place here on this earthly realm. The battle was costly and many people perished to the fires of torment. The neutralising water from this area was evaporated and the earth was scorched and cracked from the tremendous energy that was witnessed here.

The wisest of elders, our ancestors from thousands of years ago, understood that areas such as these held great power, making it a heritage site but forgotten by men and beast alike. His story of fantasy brings forth a memory of unlimited possibilities as I look across the ever stretching plain. A pattern seems to form from the dry cracked earth. I can't quite make out the symbol as we descend quickly then suddenly enter the deadened skyscraper-high pillars. The air is scorched with the smell and taste of sulphur, as the stars and Moon became a distant memory from what awaits me deep within the unknown.

Led through a maze of tightly knitted pillars, from when that part of the world had been submerged at the bottom of the ocean, I can see where the water had eroded and carved the maze we travelled.

"We are constantly being pursued by an opposing force" one of the monks says as we came to a resting place. This doesn't sit well with me at all. "What kind of opposing forces you ask? The ones that are in your deepest fears" but before he can finish, a signal from the leading monk suggests we move on.

We move quickly in almost total blackness of the night, with every step the ground seeming to decline gradually. As I glimpse up at the opening cracks, seeing the stars and silver Moon overhead, following fearful of the opposing forces as I see images in the shadows, fragments of light and the realisation that I am a stranger in a strange land.

Totally disorientated, I keep close to my guides who seem to be visually clear no matter how dense the darkness, as they navigate, sensing the way, while moving in complete silence so as not to give the location of our movements away. Finally stopping to catch our breath, the monk continues where he left off.

"The opposing forces are the forces that keep you bound to the worries of not succeeding, the fears that keep your mind living in the past and future, separating you from the Earth that supports your very being, and the expecting of pain when it doesn't really exist, but by accepting these opposing forces, keeps you close to your desires. It's only when you have let go of the opposing forces, when you are truly lost from the world of worry, pain and abandonment, you will mutate into a different dimension and be free from the rule of man."

Emerging from what seemed to be an eternity of darkness, the sounds of birds call out, birthing smiles on the faces that I accompany. We have made it as we step out into what is an oasis of life, song and camp fires that reflect in the running river, casting a beautiful scene from the dazzling night light. The floor littered in a thick carpet of grass while bamboo, fig trees, coconut trees and many other vegetative life forms grow beautifully from the geometric design of the living, working eco-environment.

The monk speaks of an untold story, as we walk towards the flickering flames reflecting in the river that flows through the grounds. The river is a magical river that has no beginning and no end. It flows from the musical minds of men, which keeps these lands bursting with life. The fertile lands have much life with goats, cows and other herbivores that are kept, not for their meat, but to be part of the land that fills the area in a tranquil atmosphere.

"See, there is life down here" smiles the monk, as I run my fingers through the tall grasses trying to keep up through the golden fields. The strange small buildings scattered throughout the land, with warrior statues before the paths, slightly resemble the bamboo gardens from the past evening. I feel a strong sense of honour as we set foot on the path, slowing our pace next to them. The path, smooth to the touch, funnels us past a curtain of trees, which lead to a set of descending stone stairs. The stairs descend onto a grand Victorian-like garden with geometrical patterns for plant beds and paths lit by burning torches carrying the eye to where a giant pyramid stands, hidden away from the eyes of man. It had been buried deep within the earth which opened to the night sky.

Approaching the breath-taking structure, I can see that it has been perfectly positioned as the formatted gaps within the walls create patterns which flood light to crystals and precious stones embedded in the walls. Every desiccation crack seems to map the movements of the night sky as I cast my gaze up to the opening ether. I can't believe what I am seeing as reflecting crystals in their many colours of light empower one another and flood light to the land where the buildings are erected, where the vegetation grows, breathing life to its many inhabitants, and down to the very tip of the pyramid that is a giant transparent crystal. The scene echoes the ancient texts hidden away from mankind.

Finally, we reach the end apartment. "This will be your living quarters while you are here". Before I bow to ask the warrior statue for protection while I sleep, the monk tells me that the buildings were designed for their structural strength, as cosmic energy is attracted to stronger structures within the universe. The outer structure is much different to the inside. The inside has the shape like that of a domed hexagon, half above the ground and half below, with crystals at every point. It has a calming feeling which sends me straight to sleep.

The next morning, waking from a deep invigorating sleep, completely energised I am eager to impress now that I have reached my work place! Setting foot out of the apartment, the sun is bright and the smell of the fields graces me while I stretch out. The monks that had accompanied me the previous night are awaiting my arrival in the morning sun. We greet one another as we set off down the path, looking over the vast cultivated crops.

I ask, "What is my purpose of work today?" yet the monk doesn't answer. Instead he tells me a tale of the lands we walk. These lands haven't always been so beautiful and peaceful.

"There were two powerful Gods that travelled many nights and days to a calling that burnt in their chests. Each arrived at the point in their hearts, the two opposing forces, one from the north and the other from the south but on arrival they witnessed each other's presence. They argued claiming that this part of the Earth belonged to them, and it was their birth right. This heritage of instinct to fight for what they believed to be their right lasted many moons. Waging war on the other, a great battle with the Gods took place depicted as one giant bird and the other a snake that had monumental size. They fought incessantly over the land, the giant bird pecked the eyes out of the snake's head who developed a heat sense vision. The snake ripped the tail from the bird making it impossible to navigate in the air, so the bird grew a giant golden tail. But one another were an equal match, finally coming to an agreement for the bird to take the skies where the seeds from distant plant life would be carried in by the bird while the snake would use its infra-red vision to flush out the mice that lived in the tall grasses. See, the heritage wasn't just of the land, it was to meet one another and share their hearts, no more did they have to struggle and the land fell into a peaceful reality."

As we talk, walking toward the centre of the gardens, we are met by an old man dressed in robes. The man in the robes and I continue to approach the pyramid's entrance as the monks follow ten feet behind. Either side of the path are monks holding different stances. I ask why they use so many stances. The man answers, pointing to a submissive stance, "This one helps you let go of control and fear", then pointing to another stance, "This one is a power stance and it allows you to gain power and confidence, dissolving deeper levels of ego."

"It's a lot like yoga!" The man in turn acknowledges my words then continues. "Through using the body you observe what activates different energetic emotions. We can then help to create and manifest a chosen desire. For you to know what your body wants to express, by bringing an understanding and awareness to it, we then express ourselves freely."

By this time we have covered the length of the gardens and are standing before the pyramid's mouth, where two giant stone birds stand. The birds are the same as the bird I saw at the bamboo gardens and now here. The monk noticed my regressive look. "Phoenix is her name. She represents rebirth to whoever observes her existence."

Entering, the monk that had studied in India is called forth.

"This is your Yogi," I am instructed, "and he will be leading you on your spiritual journey from here on out."

I feel very comfortable in my yogi's presence, as we have become accustomed to one another. The inside of the pyramid is hollow and bright in colour, with the walls tapering up to a giant transparent crystal at its apex. In the middle of the open space stands a coiling staircase that leads to a flat circular platform, one third of the pyramid's height. As we advance towards the structure, the monk begins in his teachings.

"A God-man, Om Shanti, a 'peaceful life', I was told by a dimensional shifting traveller. How do I know this, because words change all things when accepted? My journey throughout India seemed to be a rite of passage. I seemed to be encountering sought-out individuals naturally. These beings say I have saved them! How is it that I, with all my contortions, 'free' or rescue such influential beings? Questions swarm around my mind. Who am I to be such a being, for these beings to wait so long in their lives, for me to arrive?"

I find myself guided by these enthusiastic people to ancient temples of practice. They are keen to show me their devotees. They are keen to pave passages through gates of many. 'Follow me' they say. Why would these sought-out people, particular individuals, embrace me in all that the ancestors are? I am in the subtlest of ways becoming freer as I share time with such humans. They are a peculiar race of realm swappers. Their worlds seem to ask for tribute or sacrifice to travel. Either death is needed to reach a gate or proving identity to reach holy realms. I, for one, am still interested in this world!

We walk around to the base of the natural staircase where many people are sat on the floor facing inward toward the centre and we begin to climb the steps one at a time. The hand rail had been carved and seems to resemble scales, while it spirals upward leading the anticipation to what awaits.

Engrossed in the conversation, I barely notice the column that the staircase and scaly handrail wraps around. Finding ourselves perched on the platform's surface, several people meditate, a feeling that I am surrounded by friends whelms within me. I notice that the floor has been made of stone with patterns of interlocking triangles. As I sit in guided meditation, my yogi begins.

"Meditating in the Taj Mahal gave me the sense of the loss of a true loved Goddess. The beating heart is still felt in the walls of this tribute. I, for one, quickly realised that the love present brought forth, loss, suicide, despair, grasping at the tunnelling harmonies of the stars, a realisation. That realisation was a wish, a wish that was to love all the same. This made complete sense! Only true love is felt, truly felt, when there is no separation, only truth! Truth in that love is equal to be in that space in every moment opens the flower of the heart. The heart then can truly be free and the soul is released to express."

Frustration takes a hold of me and I shout out, "I cannot do this, I cannot live in the eternal endurance of the moment, it's too painful." A hand touches the knee that throbs with the pain that eleven hours of sitting crystallized brings. The hand holds no judgment, which instantly settles my mind, and the voice then speaks, "If we endure these times, we fuse the future that our evolutionary generations exist in. Be patient as the madness will subside, trust in your teachings.

You are not what you think you are. The personalities are a screen to a limited perception of existence. We hold onto the idea of knowing oneself. This gives us purpose. But sadly you are not that existence. You are not, and never have been. So what are we if not a collection of thoughts and feelings that make up the functioning personalities and characters? We are nothing and everything.

The question is what would you like to be? This knowledge of subject matter has spun the greatest of minds a yarn of manifestation on the limitless scale. If this is obvious, then why are we not seeing this? Why are we holding onto false ideals, of not just wants but ourselves? The answer is nothing. 'Nothing', it seems like a simple answer, doesn't it?"

> Nothing is a something, we see as a nothing.
> This nothing becomes the limitation.
> See nothing as a something.
> Then something will appear out of nothing.
> Step out of the shadows.

As the days fall upon blankets of stars, the words from my teachings ring true in the exercises I practice religiously in the early mornings. As the sun floods the land, awakening the plant life, this would be the first of my meditation sittings, just before starting my day, as the half sleep state has a faster effect to approaching the 'no thoughts' state. Sometimes I become overpowered by the sensation of drifting in and out of the other plains, and I fall back to sleep. I soon realise that if I don't succumb to temptation with sleep, I can meditate and not need sleep at all. The state of conscious sleep, 'no thought' state, gives me the chemical balance along with the deep levels of REM, which one needs in order sufficiently to recharge the physical being.

In fact, the levels of conscious meditation bring forth a new awareness, along with a faster wit and reactions to the earthly realms. The days seem to be eternal when I practice my observations during meditation, and then they fly by when I let my auto pilot take the helm. It seems that I am in two worlds, split like a reflection as I regress unknowingly, then snap out of the thought world, realising my mind has wandered off the beaten track.

The many people that I have become accustomed to, welcome me with tales of ancestral inspirations, as dance and stories were expressed around communal fires. A story of how fire symbolises rebirth and how other elements can transfer information from land to human alike. The water that passes through the mountains obtains the language of the land. The ancient information that is stored in the flowers, the many stones and sounds are transferred to the water molecules, as they are intelligent living elementals of higher ascension. Then when humans and other living beings that inhabit this earth drink the elixir, the information is transferred to the human, but as the water becomes trapped and funnelled through distributing pipes etc., the information gets lost and the people forget about the lands and our ancient traditions.

On the fourth day I have come to know all the domesticated beasts that wander the cultivated landscape, all the characters of the many charismatic people, and have lost the notion that I have been sent to work in a distant country. This time of comfort has yet to pass, as the time has come to take me beyond the sanctuary of the apartment where I slept, and the water that I drank, far beyond and much deeper into the hot humid caverns of the slowly moving rocks that I sensed beneath.

My spiritual guide and I seem to walk aimlessly for hours before finding ourselves in a cave of crystals that look luminescent.

"This is where we rest before you embark on your soul journey." he says, looking across the space to an opening in the wall pointing, "That is where your opposing forces await your soul journey. We will rest here while I prepare you for what you must hold as a constant."

My nerves seem to jump off my skin, with the knowing that I have to venture alone.

"The cave that awaits you will give you no pity and will take all if you let it consume you. You will find sorrow, hate, greed, jealousy, worry and eternal pain as you travel the path but, *such remember these words*, 'I am my senses that lead me through this journey, I trust in my senses and I accept the world around me, I feel love and beauty in the moment and I am excited to share what I have learnt with the images of perceptions as my current reality, and what I want as my experience, throughout my existence to serve a higher knowing of good harmonies".

We sit, exhausted as the day held no sustenance, while I watch the man opposite me drink and eat heartedly, without sharing a crumb. My eyes bulge and my stomach weeps with no satisfaction in sight, which brings an annoying endless quiet, as the man won't stop looking at me. His look feels pressing, like he knows an inside joke, of which I am the centre. Casting my eyes to the masses of illuminating crystals that have sharp points around me, seeming to radiate an intense wave of some kind that seems to extract the will to carry on.

My eyes slowly become less focused and my mind drifts. Suddenly the monk claps his hands, which startles me.

"Time to go" he disturbs the silence with the rustling of empty food wrappers. "Come on, come on" he eagerly says with a mouth half filled with food. The cave's entrance is circular with no warmth of fresh air coming from the evaporating water that normally accompanies such a setting. Turning to find a little reassurance but seeing nothing of the monk, a cold shiver flows through me. There is nowhere to go but forward into the darkness, breathing shallow while stepping into its mouth.

The rugged rock formation leads in what seems to be a tunnel which has no light or no sounds and no end. Shuffling my way forward, the only sound heard is my quivering breathing as the tunnel is cold and the sounds from my feet seem to progressively get louder. The cave's night accompanies a new brilliant light, the light of sound. By listening to the sounds that echo past my following steps, an idea of direction shines ablaze. With my eyes wide, the tunnel takes the form of sound waves, echoing onward, sensing the distance through uncertainty.

The unrelenting darkness seems to bring my body to a heightened state of sensory perception. With every slight sound I feel my ears adjusting, left then right, with the smell and taste of the little rising dust that had settled throughout the years. The saddening sharp sounds start to play tricks on my mind, with the images of senior school, ex-lovers and erotic fancies. I try to block them out, trying to keep the task in hand but the flashing images of many past experiences keep swirling around my mind. I try to focus with my eyes but the pitch blackness has nothing to focus on, while the pounding of last conversations I had, the job that I could have done better, the times and moments when I acted out of character, the reliving actions of my embarrassments toy with my mind and knot my stomach. Why did I do that? That isn't like me, if anyone found out, stop it, please, no, the bills haven't been paid, I haven't given the people around me enough attention, and they will not stay around if I don't appease their needs. "Why, why, why am I here?" I scream as the sounds of my voice carry down the echoing passageway. I think about turning back but the disorientation of the continuing images in my mind has me lost. I sit on the cold floor hugging my legs, trying to find some kind of solace.

Suddenly the monk's image appears before me and a sentence re-births within me: "The nature of the self is to observe the world around you, and this is done by observing the breath".

I centre myself, knowing that I am the senses of energies that lead me through this journey. I begin to say aloud, "I trust in my senses and I accept the world around me, I feel love and beauty in the moment and I am excited to share what I have learnt with the harmonic images of my current reality, and what I want as my experience for higher good throughout my existence of expressional harmonies."

The feeling of calm refreshes my mind and body as I observe my breathing. While listening for the distant echo that leads my way, the tunnel with its endless marching starts to lose its cylindrical shape as I steadily continue along. The sound seems to travel out to the left. With no guidance to comfort my lack of vision, my struggle to make sense of the darkness continues. Clicking my fingers sends waves of musical visions out into the space. Realising that the left hand side of the tunnel doesn't exist, I cling to the right side of the tunnel. Rustling noises come from the ceiling of the distant cave above. The right side of the tunnel has decreased in width to a thin ledge where my heels hang over the edge to the unknown descent. The panic in my voice seems to disturb the rustling sounds that came from the ceiling, making me freeze to regain my observing of the breath.

A flash of my ancestors tell me that we can hold onto revenge or many other driven pursuits to mask the face of what we truly should acknowledge, which is our suffering. When we can acknowledge by observing one's suffering, we can come out of the fires that burn in hell, and know that it is a part of our being, along with anger and rage. This knowing lets me deal and move on, but to ignore the fact it exists is to suppress and when we suppress, life can be hard and limiting.

The fluttering sounds start to turn into thousands of squeaks that roar from the ceiling of the cave. I slip and fall, just managing to grab the ledge where I stood only moments ago. The sound of panic disturbs the bats that release their rock held-tight grip, giving flight to a swarm, as I climb pulling myself to safety. The bats keep swirling around me, taking my breath, gasping for air whilst screaming, an image of the man in the robe comes to my mind. "The nature of the 'self' is to observe".

I look around the cave with my senses, giving the environment an assessment. The cave is dark, I cannot see, I have bats flying around me but now I have stopped moving around, they are not hitting me anymore. It is damp in this part of the cave, my breathing is better now as the humidity is comforting here. Calm, listening to the squeaks from the womb in this place, the whirling sounds of the bats merges as oneness, as the symphonic waves pierce the very fragments of the being I am, tearing a hole of awareness of total welcoming within my consciousness. After a while the bats fly out, leaving me to my thoughts as I continue to observe the once fluttering cave. Now all I had to do to be able to get out of there was to sense my way by using my voice to create an echo, in which I can make a path.

Making my way through the tunnel, a tiny speck of light flashes ahead in-between my eyebrows. This light is very bright but accompanied with the sounds of singing birds that channelled down the tunnel's exit. The light grows in diameter automatically following my musical song, which guided me for so long. The smell and taste of the air makes me rush towards the exit, exhaustedly stopping, looking in wonder. Returning back to my natural self I walk, listening once again in harmony. The light is bright but welcoming finally stepping out of the cave's mouth. I feel at home in the daylight, with a sense that everything has changed but stayed the same. The mountains and trees had grown in meaning as I could see that they had arrived to their most evolutionary state, the blue sky with flickering light particles that danced overhead in high resolution, and the wind's rhythmical music seemed to breathe as it carried life with every inhalation.

Stepping forward, my foot touches the ground. My body automatically balances itself as I walk, my legs re-adjusting as the ground is uneven taking my next step. Marvelling in wonder, my eyes pan across, focusing from the once darkness. There ahead stand three monks and the man in a robe, awaiting my birth from the cave's heart. Approaching the familiar smiling faces, they appear to be glowing with a light of aura searching out for all to see. Drawing my look back to where I stand, I notice my hand glowing with this same light.

The man in the robe smiles, seeming to repeat a sentence that once touched him as an old man's apprentice: "As soon as you let go of the fact that we live in the observer's world, and stop continuing to expect pain or worry from a limited experience, you release fear and start living from the energetic body which you have achieved. Well done, now you are ready for the next stage!"

We sit for a while as the sun sets. Walking back through the light of the night doesn't seem to be night at all, the night seems as plain as day!

Entering the pyramid once again, all seems to have changed. The feeling of enchantment flutters in the atmosphere, and the resolution has richness in depth. Ascending the crystal sturdy staircase, I step one foot in front of the other with the sense of music and light in every movement like that of ancient times birthing in me. Here with an open heart I stand, seeming to have missed so much detail from the last time I ascended the spiral staircase, as now the handrail is solid gold and the stones laid at the top of the platform are made of interlocking jade stone triangles.

The jade had evolved to its highest evolutionary state, along with the solid gold handrail and 12 small gold Phoenix bird statues that perch on the handrail, making up the perimeter of the platform. Now I can see the faces of the other beings for what they are. They don't look human at all, more like mythical beings from fairytale stories. Suddenly, I can't stop smiling, for I have been given the chance to love so deeply, that it has burnt all of the karma and fear away, not just in myself, but all that so happened to be in my presence.

You see, we are subjected to hiding our true selves, *realms,* not purposely but through fear! I see that even the gifted of sages, gurus etc suffer from the division of realm merging. A bridge of light becomes inaccessible because a filter is, or becomes, the reality. It seems to me that there is a dual co-existence that blinds us to limited harmonious expression. Tunnelling deeper into meditation, I found oneness, a desire to leave my body and mutate, the feeling of welcoming with a healthy invite, to what I now know as home.

Experiencing the divine realms of loving welcoming continues to grow and expand within, while I walk the Earth. I am one with it, and one is one with me. To bring that, what so happens to be my ultimate expression, holds a little smile on my face and in my soul because I am indeed still here! Still here for what exactly? Maybe to express such a moment with the realm of the humans, witches, fairies, alchemists, wizards etc. A world of vision and uncertainty awaits my ever growing humbleness. Now know this the monk spoke, "To surround yourself with objects or life forms that are at their most evolutionary state of form, you indeed evolve alongside with them."

I felt the evolutionary steps towards all realms as the weight of his words rang true.

Sitting, finding my place amongst the meditation circle, feeling humble, I close my eyes to begin my further teachings, transcendental consciousness births in me naturally. I have earned the right to be activated by the Elders amongst the group, being humble beings alongside myself. Effortlessly, as I find trust and community with new eyes, hearing and the heart of awakening connection to one soul of true self, I feel the sensation of floating upward toward a shining line of light. This line seems to connect to my earthly body and my original soul of pure consciousness.

Travelling along this umbilical cord, I see many joyous pastimes reflected in passing fields, where children play with the wildlife and families and friends joyously play water games. Rejoicing in these memories holds an anchor for love in such realms. Suddenly, with travelling melodies of a mythical harp playing strings, beautiful warmth makes me float past my apartment window where I see my sister tending to my turtle with the courteousness of a novice baby holder, with the truth of love in a true family tie. Ascending up past then into the city, I see my 42nd floor office workplace. Passing, I smile in the knowledge of this choice, thinking to where I truly want to serve as the expressions I so wish to inspire in other people and a future family if so blessed to grace my life.

The anchor of light seems to guide me with an increasing loving energy. Like music to my ears, it calls me into the park, this little treasure in the city, smelling the grasses as I skip upon the surface of the lake waters. Seeing my body upon the hillside, a thrill bursts in the soul that I am, floating closer to my crystallised slumbering body of expression I drift into a fluttering childlike heart and open my eyes.

I see that I never left the park at all! All is well in the world, I thought, as I slowly walk to where my chariot awaits so patiently. Hearing the melody of such elemental experiences, looking up to where the sun shines through the trees, cascading beams of coloured light in a picturesque backdrop enters me. I appreciate the moment as I see a friendly familiar face in the place where I saw the shadow earlier.

"Chloe is that you?" As we stand close, she smiles and we chat comfortably for some time outside of work hours. Exchanging personal details, I travel back to my apartment with a smile in my heart. I give a wave to the passing neighbours as I enter my air-conditioned apartment with a breath of relief as I sit contently, consciously, at my solid oak desk, inspired, *I write this book* with my friend, my turtle.

Water

The elixir of life. The origin of life. From the humble workings of Abiogenesis, the sustaining of the ecosystem and its advanced applications it is the closest thing we have to liquid magic. Water is necessary and abundant in nearly all forms. Its applications are forever in use with more discoveries concerning its potential. Here is a list of facts:

Hydropower is the world's most used renewable energy source that does not pollute the environment and is 95% efficient. It has been in use for 1000s of years in varying systems. The amount of water on our planet has remained the same for 2 billion years and the only substance naturally occurring in solid, liquid or gas form. Frozen water is 9% lighter than water. Water regulates the temperature of the planet.

Water consists of three atoms, two Hydrogen and one Oxygen that bond together via an electrical charge. Its chemical formula is written H_2O. 66% of the human body consists of water, all our organs are rich in water and it is transported to fulfil our bodily functions. The healthy human brain is 75% water. Human bones 25%. Blood 83%. We can live a month without food but less than a week without water. Water is used to regulate the temperature of the human body. That of course applies before transcendental consciousness. After the bridge is made to transcendental awareness and pure truth the possibilities are endless.

Water is also a medium for bacteria, be they healthy or otherwise, heat, light, sound and electricity. As mentioned in previous chapters, water also produces negative ions when it crashes or creates waves, the benefits of these ions are numerous and necessary.

In the realm of spirituality it is a medium to psychic realms. It is highly resonant to thought and according to Mr Masaru Emoto he has come to the conclusion music and thought affect the structure of water molecules. Minimal thoughts or intentions such as "Love" created perfect symmetrical patterns akin to snowflakes, whilst "Anger" produced odd, malformed shapes. This way of thinking is supposed to enhance the quality of the water that lives as a percentage within our Earthly emitting bodies. It is not a new concept!

Mediums and more commonly Priests often bless water to imbue it with psychic power or the power of Christ in the latter case. Scientifically speaking not much evidence upholds either example. Some argue it is a self-belief of what you put in, you get out. Through chanting and likewise actions, we learn exactly how to bring into reality, the healthiest of transcendental water to drink.

Over the last 20 years water has been found to have extensive properties as a fuel via a unique form of electrolysis. The bond between the Hydrogen atoms and Oxygen atom are separated. The Hydrogen is then burnt to use fuel. This can be written as HHO, and its applications could replace virtually all current forms of fuel.

Infamously Stephen Meyers, who was working out of his garage, invented and patented the first unique water powered engine, or Water Fuel Cell. It could run on any kind of water, including rain, salt, tap, non-drinking and drinking water, ice and snow melted down. Using the electrolysis noted above, he calculated that if he took his dune buggy from Los Angeles to New York, he would use around 22 gallons of water. This is unprecedented. A gallon of oil on average can take you 25 miles. The distance from Los Angeles to New York is 2778 miles, which means an average of 125 miles per gallon of water.

John Kanzius who was a former radio technician may have a slant on sound affecting water. He is burning salt water using radio waves, which he is testing to kill cancer cells. By using very particular frequencies, Kanzius was able to separate the bond between the Hydrogen and Oxygen. By finding the resonant frequency of the water, he can make a flame that burnt at over 3000 degrees Fahrenheit. His machines also desalinize salt water. In theory, boats would never have to refuel as the very substance they travel upon would be the fuel.

His work on curing cancer, via direct injection of metallic nanoparticles into a cancerous tumour and burning them inside the body with radio waves is also something of interest.

Another pioneer of the water fuel phenomenon, which should rather be an industry, is Denny Klein. Using his own form of electrolysis, he designed a welder that is warm to the touch yet against inorganic materials becomes hotter than the surface of the sun, melting brass balls and cutting sheet metal. When put against other materials, the gas returns back to water. He is also another advocate of using just water to power his car, using only 4 ounces to travel 100 miles.

There are even devices that can purify Water almost instantaneously, serving a dire need in countries with poor access to clean drinking water. Of the 3% of the world's drinking water, only a 3rd of the world has access to it.

Water it seems is the most necessary, malleable, powerful source of energy and information exchange known to us. It is the very thing that gave birth to us, evolved us, sustains us, sustains the planet, and can solve our energy usage.

Note if the water used through marvels of technological advances doesn't evaporated back into the environment, we could have a very serious problem within the world.

The river brings tears to the cheeks of the innocent past-times. If only I know where to sit alongside the flowing riverside, to the fountain of youth and longevity!

Looking around to my left, it reminds me of here, then slowly taking my gaze to the right, becomes there! Time I take to feel the inner most workings of fragmented time passed and distant! But still I sit here with rosy cheeks, as the tear's roll down my face.

Thank you to all that have shown your true colours. Thank you for such an audience, and thank you, as I live amongst you, consciously apart of this great design!

Thank you,

John Gihair

Life is indeed a music lesson. Depending on what keys of musical rhythmical harmonics you press, they guide you! A base like fashion or that of a higher octave expression! But really, life is about the rising and falling of richness entwined within the game play of both hands, in this dual co-existence of consciousness.

If you can save me, I can save you, in the consciousness of discovery.

Notes

It is easy to open a door, but a door that has been opened for you, that has torn through the fabric of your known reality so you can be seen and heard, is that of a great strength, a great gift and a great belonging.

I do indeed wish you a comfortable read ahead. This book, my journey across the great continents of this beautiful, habitable planet Earth was in search of my life's manual. Truth be told, the initial thought of desire is the start and the finishing line. *There is no separation.* It's only the journey toward the so called finish that can spin us into a beehive.

My warmest appreciation.
John Gihair

My beliefs are not to focus just on the scientific rule of law within the universe; I believe you should infuse your chosen religious spiritual beliefs with findings that I will explain in this book, to give you a greater understanding, and to empower your spiritual religious beliefs by discovering deeper messages that already exist within your chosen manuscripts. (Page 1)

By learning dietary solutions to be able to conform within society, and leave the primal self forever we can, of course, not suppress but release this hunger/ thirst type of appetite. (Page 6)

Rebellion can take the form of the simplest of things and can stay with you for a life time, or life times! As soon as you can distinguish where your life path truly belongs, down the middle, your mother's life will fall away and so will your father's, thus your true path will be shown and the potential energy that was held back by old conscious beliefs will flow into your very existence. (Page 9)

To stand up and be counted is something my childhood taught me! It also taught me to be part of a social grouping, to be part of a community, to unite within my skin and feel settled beyond doubt. (Page 11)

If part of our soul search is to re-program DNA by diet, speech etc, imagine what consciousness we will obtain if we process light from distant stars (Moon bathe) that are filtered down through our retinas into the body! (Page 13)

For you to find yourself is the truest legacy to leave, and as you do this it paves the way for others to follow in your frequency footprints. (Page 17)

Studies show that our energetic emotions are indeed governed by the movements of orbiting celestial planets, which affect the electromagnetic fields within us. So, by knowing this, at times of planetary alignment or full Moon cycles, meditation, with the most innocent of intentions, helps serve to increase our electromagnetic attraction. (Page 24)

This doesn't mean I am separate from external beings. It simply means that I am becoming more consciously aware of not-so-present elements already conscious in my conscious heart! It's a trigger to see the bigger picture, if you will. (Page 27)

When we re-associate, birthing appreciation in richness, becoming transcendental or not, it matters not as there are many levels of happiness, and many life-times to experience, expand and try anew! Life is indeed about richness, a tasteful variety of depth in quality gives us our unique quirks on life. Embrace these keys of musical notes of life's riches. We can mirror expression, playing alongside, or trust in 'all is well!'. Your choice! (Page 32)

Let us play outside as much as possible to benefit from the proximity of water and sunshine. (Page 34)

By learning the nature of our environments, internal and external we keep our glass just so slightly empty for us to constantly receive. (Page 36)

In many popular bestsellers, meaning manuscripts, tapestries, paintings, etc. where God is portrayed as the infinite and the human being is portrayed as having infinite potential!
Infinite potential is the ability to know that your current conscious mind will attract information that, "DOES NOT" already exist in your awareness! This means that a progression of a thought evolves and manifests into your reality. Your reality is the observations of awareness. (Page 40)

Remember we are governed to live within an imbalanced frequency thus one forms highs and lows. (Page 43)

Be with all, in the best of intentions. Feel this within your belly, warmth in your belly, *expanding* forever growing forever into warmth. Then ask the universe for your wish.
Accept this. Now by letting it go of all limitations of ideology, dreams or wishing, feel welcome in your skin, heart, breath, planet and equanimity. (Page 51)

People that have been lucky enough to observe 'love', have learnt the magic tricks to life; using these laws for their bidding. We use them every day on a miniscule scale and of course on a much larger scale. (Page 51)

When a legend is born, people take notice. When a great leader dies, people take notice. When you find a burst of beautiful energy that holds you in the arms of effortlessness, you take notice. Take notice! (Page 55)

So there I sat for five years. With eyes closed for days at a time, with my twelve hour barbell sessions and my sitting in the box splits for what seemed to be eternity, I sat, and I sat some more with no friction or concept of time! (Page 59)

See that there! That is a magical door. When you entered you learnt all you will ever need to know from here on out! When you leave, you have the choice of what universe you live within. Choose well, and live a happy life. Imagination and magic is another key. (Page 64)

The actions that were out of character can be cast aside, as you know who you are now and will forever be you. Fear is to fear itself, so if we know that fear isn't part of our true selves, then free we are. Love life is another key to healing. (Page 67)

The present is now, regression was then and the future is the next sentence you choose to read. To be able to be as true to oneself as possible we must look at instinct. (Page 68)

Looking at the many levels that make up an individual, teaches us to let go of the programming that was inherited through teachings otherwise not in line with oneself and to propels us into an informational world of whatever you want it to be. The pen is in your hand, the future is yourself and how exact you wish it to be. (Page 70)

Very seldom do we let others lead us into self-discovery through their actions. The observer's world is awaiting you. We must bring all forces into existence, all of our characters as oneness, to unite the spark of creativity. (Page 73)

Remember that life is a game that is played with the cards of energies that blinds us with a false visual binding! Belief in magic is another key! (Page 80)

Try to be there for your partner as you expand together. (Page 82)

One hundred days of celibacy to build a foundation is said to build enough Qi or Chi to convert into Shen which indeed helps you on the journey of enlightenment. (Page 90)

Once the ego is gone, a Chi is able to flow uninhibited. The mind and body are the same thing. In Chinese philosophy, the mind and the heart are also the same thing; there are no divisions, only those made by men. Everything is in sway, when Yang rises to its peak it becomes Yin and vice versa. Like the Law of Conservation of Energy, nothing is destroyed, only transformed. (Page 92)

Staring at the cloudless blue sky above, the smell of the fresh air and the heat of the Sun on your skin, you thank Titan, the God of the sea, for your life and the world that you just witnessed. *Breathing is key.* (Page 96)

'Memorize, memorize, mesmerize. Memorize, memorize, mesmerize!'
(Page 97)

Try and remember to use your name in conjunction with uplifting phrases. Treat your name as sacred, because it is. When addressing or introducing, treat other people's names in the same way. Never use them without attaching to them some positive emotions. (Page 101)

Many ancient cultures around the world have independently discovered and formulated inks for the purposes of writing and drawing. We don't all arrive at the discovery at the same time. Most of us are lost in battle of continuous cycles for generations, but knowing that the many routes that have guided the Elders on their stages of conscious awareness are laid bare, you can observe and free yourself as the creational beings that *YOU* are. (Page 103)

A mighty ancient flowing river that was forged by the hand of the Supreme Being can indeed be stopped by a dam and redirected with the engineering of creational individuals! With the river newly redirected, it finds itself at the exact destination, the sea or oceans. Do not think you are too old or too settled to continue with what you forged, but then got held up at a dam or pit stop; energy just wants to flow *so let it be*. You believe in YOU remember. (Page 108).

Nothing is a something, we see as a nothing.
This nothing becomes the limitation.
See nothing as a something.
Then something will appear out of nothing.
Step out of the shadows. (Page 123)

I enter my air-conditioned apartment with a breath of relief as I sit contently, consciously, at my solid oak desk, inspired, *I write this book* with my friend, my turtle. (Page 128)

Note if the water used through marvels of technological advances doesn't evaporated back into the environment, we could have a very seriously problem within the world. (Page 131)

Thank you to all that have shown your true colours. Thank you for such an audience, and thank you, as I live amongst you, consciously apart of this great design! (Page 132)

Thank you,

John Gihair

Bibliography

Aiello, L. C. (1995, 4). The Expensive-Tissue Hypothesis. Retrieved 8 29, 2011, from Current Anthropology: http://www.jstor.org/pss/2744104.

Asia Society. (2011). Belief Systems Along the Silk Roads. Retrieved November 7, 2011, from http://asiasociety.org/: http://asiasociety.org/countries/trade-exchange/belief-systems-along-silk-roads?page=0,2

Bodsworth, J. (2003). *Childhood.* Available: http://www.reshafim.org.il/ad/egypt/people/childhood.htm. Last accessed 17th June 2014.

Boquetespa. (n.d.). Health Benefits of a vacation in the mountains. Retrieved September 6, 2011, from Boqueteaspa.com: http://boquetespa.com/health-benefits-of-a-vacation-in-the-mountains/

Bosman, A. (2008). DMT (Dimethyltryptamine). Retrieved 2011, from issuu: http://issuu.com/scottjenson/docs/ananda_bosman_-_on_dmt_and_the_pine

Celestrial Healing. (n.d.). Vegetarianism "The Mental Benefits". Retrieved 9 24, 2011, from http://www.celestialhealing.net/celestialhomepage.htm: http://www.celestialhealing.net/mentalveg2.htm

Coon, R. (n.d.). Infinity Ley. Retrieved August 12, 2011, from Earth Chakras: http://earthChakras.org/Infinity-Ley.php

Dickenson, I. P. (1993-2011). The Discovery of Schumann Resonance. Retrieved August 12, 2011, from Earth Breathing: http://www.earthbreaking.co.uk/sr.htm

Einstein, A. (1905). Does the Inertia of a Body Depend upon its Energy Content? *Annalen der Physik.* 18: 639-641.

Hanks, T. (2005, May 22). Tom Hanks' Four Percent Solution. Retrieved October 7, 2011, from Plantea.com: http://www.plantea.com/Tom-Hanks.htm

health-benefit-of-water.com. (2011). Water Generates Negative Ions. Retrieved August 30, 2011, from Health Benefit of Water: http://www.health-benefit-of-water.com/negative-ions.html

HealthCare Medicine Institute. (2012, May 30). University of Maryland Acupuncture Research - It Works! Retrieved June 9, 2012, from HealthCMI: http://www.healthcmi.com/index.php/acupuncturist-news-online/558-marylandacupunctureceusworks

Hagelin, J. S. (1993, 7). Effects of Group Practice of the Transcendental Meditation Program on Preventing Violent Crime in Washington, DC: Results of the National Demonstration Project, June–July 1993. Retrieved 2 5, 2012, from Maharishi University of Management: http://www.mum.edu/m_effect/dc_md.html

König, H.L. (1979). 'Bioinformation, Electrophysical Aspects'. In: Electromagnetic Bioinformation, Popp, F.A., Becker, G., König, H.L., Peschka, W., (eds), Urban a nd Schwarzenberg, p-25.

Mann, D. (2002, May 6). Negative Ions Create Positive Vibes. Retrieved September 6, 2011, from WebMD: http://www.webmd.com/balance/features/negative-ions-create-positive-vibes

Narby, J. (n.d.). Photons. Retrieved 08 29, 2011, from FUSION Anomoly: http://fusionanomoly.net/photons.html

Pétrélis, F., Fauve, S., Dormy, E. and Valet, J-P. (2009). Simple Mechanism for Reversals of Earth's Magnetic Field. *Physical Review Letters.* 102, 144503. See: http://phys.org/news159704651.html#jCp.

Plato (1968). *Plato's Republic*. 2nd ed. United States of America: Allan Bloom. 425-439. Trans. Allan Bloom. See: http://www.inp.uw.edu.pl/mdsie/Political_Thought/Plato-Republic.pdf

Strassman, R. (2001). DMT, The Spirit Molecule. Inner Traditions Bear and Company.

Moss, T. (1981). The Body Electric, A Personal Journey Into the Mysteries of Parapsychology and Kirlian Photography. Liverpool: Granada Publishing Limited.

U.S. Department of Agriculture. (2010). Dietry Guidelines for Americans 2010. Retrieved: 2011, from www.health.gov.org: http://www.health.gov/dietaryguidelines/dga2010/dietaryguidelines2010.pdf

Van der Broek, R (1972), *The Myth of the Phoenix*, Seeger, I. Trans. Brill, E.J.

Vorly, E. (2014). Brainwave Guide. Available: http://www.themeditationsolution.com/brainwaveguide.htm. Last accessed 17th June 2014.

Wang, C. (2004). The Effect of Tai Chi on Health Outcomes in Patients With Chronic Conditions. A Systematic Review. *Arch Intern Med.* 164, 493-501.

Wicherink, J. (2006). The mysterious DNA. Retrieved 8 29, 2011, from Souls of Distortion: http://www.soulsofdistortion.nl/SODA_chapter9.html.

Index

Abiogenesis, xiii, 128
Acupuncture, 22, 90, 91
Alpha rhythms, 23, 35
Ankermueller, Dr, 23
Balance, xii, xiv, 5, 15, 16, 17, 18, 24, 39, 45, 90, 122, 136
Beta, 48
Bird, Dr Harvey, 46
Body Electric, The, 90, 136
Buddha, 74, 86, 87, 88
Buddhist, 16, 45
Chakras
  Base Chakra, 11, 29, 32, 60, 61, 73, 81, 102, 103
  Crown Chakra, 11, 29, 31, 63, 78, 81, 104, 105
  Earth Chakras, 22, 136
  Sacred Sacrum Chakra, 11, 31, 32, 61, 74, 81, 97, 102, 103
  Third Eye Chakra, 31, 63, 77, 81, 104
  Throat Chakra, 31, 62, 77, 81, 103, 104
  Vortex, 71
channelling, 70, 96, 102, 104
Chanting, 16, 45, 60, 86, 98, 128
Chi, 16, 17, 89, 90, 91, 112, 115, 133
  Ki, 90
  Orgone energy, 90
  Prana, 90
Creationists, xiii
Cycles, 1, 3, 4, 9, 11, 25, 26, 39, 40, 65, 66, 67, 101, 103, 104, 110, 132, 134
  Improper, 5
Da Vinci, Leonardo, xiv
Daedalus, 82
Dark Energy, xiii, 15
Dark Matter, xiii, 15
Delta, 48
Dimethyltryptamine, 43
Dmitri, xiii
DNA, xiv, 7, 8, 9, 11, 14, 20, 36, 42, 43, 65, 77, 85, 86, 131, 136
  cellular metabolism, 8
  codons, 7, 8, 9
  human genome, 7
  molecule, 7, 8
Earth Chakras, 22, 136
Ego, 16, 79, 91, 133
Einstein, Albert, xii, 2, 15
Electromagnetic Field, 11, 13, 23, 25, 26, 31, 56, 60, 61, 62, 75, 78, 131
Electromagnetic Spectrum, 15, 19, 29, 49
Electromagnetism, 15
Elementals, 25, 80, 86, 89, 122
Energy points, 11, 18, 29, 62, 79
Epsilon, 47, 49
Evolution, xiii, xiv, 5, 13, 36, 100
Father Sky, 11, 76
Feng Shui, 22, 34, 36, 90
Fibonacci Sequence, xiv
Fibonacci, Leonardo, xiv
Fight or Flight, 68, 69
Gamma, 15, 47
Ghandi, 46
Ghandi, Mahatma, 46
Golden Mean, The, xiv, 8
Golden Ratio, The, xiv
Golden Swirl, The, xiv
Gravitation, Gravity, xiii, 15, 16, 30, 61
Hagelin, Dr. John, 84, 136
Hanks, Tom, 85, 136
Harmonics, 10, 16, 49, 86, 87, 103, 107, 130
Hindu, 45
Human Genome, 7
Jacobi, E., 24
Kabbalah, xii, xiii
Kanzius, John, 129
Kavandi, 88
Ki, 90
Konig, Herbert, 23
Kung Fu, 89, 90, 91
Labyrinth, The, 82, 83
Lambda, 47, 49
Ludwin, Dr, 23, 24
Magnetic Fields, 11, 13, 24, 25, 61
Mantra, 45

[140]

Mara, 86, 87
Mariana Trench, 92
Max Plank Institute, 24
Mayans, 25
Meditation, 9, 16, 17, 25, 30, 38, 39, 47, 48, 60, 62, 80, 81, 86, 87, 91, 96, 97, 101, 102, 107, 121, 122, 125, 126, 132
Milky Way, 14, 19
Minos, King of Crete, 82
Minotaur, The, 82
Moss, Thelma, 90, 91, 136
Mother Earth, 5, 11, 19, 61, 76, 100, 102
Mother Teresa, 51, 76
MRI, 15, 91
Murugan, 88
Newton, Sir Isaac, xiii
OM, 45, 77
Omega rhythms, 76
ONKAR, 45
Orgone energy, 90
Phoenix, 100, 102, 105, 125
Photons, 8, 11, 14, 18, 30, 36, 42, 67, 77, 78, 98, 136
Pineal Gland, 16, 17, 30, 43, 45, 60, 63, 77, 89
Prana, 90
Qi, 89, 90, 112, 133
Relativity, xiii, 15
Sacrifice, 4, 77, 85, 87, 88, 89, 120

Schreckenberg, Dr Gervasia, 46
Schumann, 23
Schumann Wave, 24
Shaolin, 16
Siddhartha, 86, 87
Silk Road, 52, 53, 54
Solar System, xii, 14
Spinoza, Barach, xiii
Stress
  Fight or Flight, 68, 69
  Stress Response, 68, 69
Sun Dance, 88
Suspension, 87
Szostak, Dr Jack, xiii
Tai Chi, 17, 91, 112, 115
Taj Mahal, 36, 121
Tamils, 88
Tantric, 45
Tesla, Nikola, 23, 49
Theta, 48
Titan, 95, 134
Vision Board, 26, 27, 28, 30, 31, 38, 56, 73, 74, 77, 78, 98, 102, 103
Vitruvian Man, xiv
Wever, Professor R., 24
Yang, 20, 23, 24, 76, 90, 91, 134
Yin, 20, 23, 24, 90, 91, 134
Yoga, 16, 90, 120
Zeroth Law of Thermodynamics, xii
Zheng, 114, 115
Zohar, The, xiii

CPSIA information can be obtained at www.ICGtesting.com
Printed in the USA
LVIW01n1113180916
505121LV00029B/287